Praise for *The Adventure of Leadership* . . .

"HAP KLOPP BRINGS A REFRESHING SENSE OF ADVENTURE TO THE AGE-OLD ART OF LEADERSHIP and the practice of management. Inspiring and practical advice from someone who's been there."
—Craig R. Hickman, partner, Hickman Forslund Marchand; author of *Creating Excellence* and *Mind of a Manager, Soul of a Leader*

"GIVES AN INSIGHT INTO THE MANY CRITICAL ISSUES ANY LEADER CONFRONTS. What Hap Klopp discusses here cannot be taught at any university and is only learned through experience."
—Ken L. Thuerbach, 1991 Entrepreneur of the Year, CEO, Alpine Log Homes

"THE MOST EXCITING AND BOLDEST BOOK I HAVE READ IN THE AREA OF LEADERSHIP."
—Larry Gianchetta, Dean, School of Business Administration, University of Montana

"HAP KLOPP IS A VOYAGER AND AN ARTIST WITH A STANFORD MBA who refused to follow the trodden path, and set out to build a business in unexplored territory. His success is the stuff of legend, and now he has written the book on the business of adventure and the adventure of business . . . A LIVELY, TELLING, SOULFUL, AND INSPIRATIONAL GUIDE."
—Richard Bangs, President, Mountain Travel-Sobek

The Adventure of Leadership

An Unorthodox Business Guide

HAP KLOPP

with Brian Tarcy

BERKLEY BOOKS, NEW YORK

THE ADVENTURE OF LEADERSHIP

A Berkley Book / published by arrangement with
Longmeadow Press

PRINTING HISTORY
Longmeadow Press edition published 1991
Berkley trade paperback edition / November 1994

ISBN: 0-425-14376-7

BERKLEY®
Berkley Books are published by The Berkley Publishing Group,
200 Madison Avenue, New York, New York 10016.
BERKLEY and the "B" design
are trademarks belonging to Berkley Publishing Corporation.

PRINTED IN THE UNITED STATES OF AMERICA

10 9 8 7 6 5 4 3 2 1

To businesses that are fun,
To adventures not yet begun.

CONTENTS

▲

ACKNOWLEDGMENTS

No expedition or grand adventure succeeds without a tremendous amount of support—support generally unseen by the outside world. I would like to thank everyone who has given me support in my outdoors, business and writing ventures.

First and foremost, I want to thank my family which has supported me through the peaks and valleys of my personal odysseys and quixotic adventures: Margot, unarguably the world's best mother; and Kelly and Matt who carry on my joy of life, my optimism and my irreverence. My mother, Dolores, and my brother, Kip, provided the love, inspiration, and foundation that has allowed me to take the risks.

There have been literally thousands of people who have taught, encouraged, and helped me scale the heights: Clyde Skeen (the best businessman I ever met), Dick Dewey, Allen Culver, Rob Salomon, John LeCompte, Jay Ward, Tom Applegate, Bob Gorton, Peter Glen and Keiji Urushibara. And then there are Becky, Wade, Mandy, Cynthia, Nick, Molly, Mark, Charlie, Angel, Dieter, Ted, Rich, Phil, etc., etc., etc.

I also wish to thank Doug and Susie Tompkins who started The North Face—as a retail entity with stores in San Francisco and Palo Alto. (They later went on to found and run ESPRIT.) It was those stores which I purchased that provided the base for The North Face wholesale product line which I originated.

In the adventuring and business realm all of those remarkably motivated, unbelievable, awe-inspiring people I mention in the book deserve accolades, as do R.D. Caughran and Gordon McFadden.

Finally, the biggest contribution to this book was by Brian and Debbie Tarcy who simultaneously birthed the manuscript and their twin daughters, risking tranquility and security for something they believed in. Mike Snell, an agent who ably guided me, and Daniel Bial, a senior editor who cared, have been a tremendous help. And there are all the unseen but essential players at Longmeadow Press who helped my voice to find its way into this book.

To all of you I say a heartfelt thanks.

—HK

PREFACE

▲

I am in love with the extraordinary. The company I founded, The North Face of Berkeley, California, epitomized this passion. I started the company in 1968, two years after receiving my MBA from Stanford. From the beginning The North Face—a maker of quality outdoor equipment for mountaineers, backpackers, skiers, and professional adventurers—came to represent my vision. For 20 years I disobeyed business conventions of passionless management by immersing myself in my work and, more important, in the lives and dreams of my coworkers. I told them of my dream, of my vision to be the best. And then I asked for their help.

Together we grew. We brought more people in, and we shared the vision further.

The North Face was named after the north side of any mountain, such as Eiger Mountain or the Matterhorn in Switzerland—the side exposed to the harshest elements of nature. It is considered the greatest challenge for any climber. The name was appropriate—since we knew what we wanted wouldn't be easy.

But we knew one other thing—if we pulled together, we could climb the north face of business, and it would be a hell of a lot of fun to do it.

Mine was a fascinating business. Because we made the best equipment in the world, I was constantly approached by professional adventurers who needed to be outfitted. These began as business relationships. But, as all successful relationships do, they evolved into much more. Through friendships with these people as well as my business relationships, I watched as vision became reality and risk became reward. I was moved by their energy. Always they helped sharpen my focus.

I brought these lessons into my business, and I shared them with my employees. For years my evangelical crusade was focused on my own company and periodically speaking from podiums. Recently I sold my company and tried to observe the world of business from a different perspective, that of a consultant. The perspective has changed, but my view hasn't.

I see an ever-growing crisis—a critical lack of passionate leadership. It seems everyone knows how to manage. Few know how to lead. There is such a fear of risk and a lack of joy in the working lives of most Americans that it seems impossible to expect anything but more of the same—interminable mediocrity.

That's why I felt compelled to write this book. *The Adventures of Leadership* begins at the peak of your spiritual backbone, where a single, raw nerve ending glows with the essence of life. I have written this book with precisely that part of you in mind. I want to touch the part of you that dreams of extraordinary things.

By sharing my experiences and some of the insights I've been able to glean from personal adventures both in and out of business, I hope to offer not merely ways of helping your bottom line but also ways to improve your total outlook. Certainly the intellectual cross training I have had from the variety of activities I have done and the weird and wonderful assortment of adventuring and business friends I have collected have given me some insights into what it takes to succeed against the odds in any pioneering adventure: business, sport, education, or personal.

My hope is that this book will be a real catalyst for dynamic change. It is a call to action for the disenchanted who are being stifled by corporate America and to those who are mistakenly intimidated from speaking out by an illogical reverence for managers and corporate shibboleths. I offer you my experience, my knowledge, and my instincts. I offer you my heart.

1

SWIMMING IN EMBALMING FLUID:

The Living Death of Bad Business

In 1966, I walked irreverent and happy into the middle of corporate America. I didn't stay long.

I had just received my MBA from Stanford University. This was back when an MBA was actually something useful. I thought the culture of a major corporation might be beneficial, but as I began to interview around, I quickly learned that irreverence and happiness were not exactly typical or approved corporate qualities.

I didn't really know what I wanted, but I sure knew what I didn't want, and unfortunately that was all I could find. Blandness. Fear of risk. Fear of change. Everywhere I looked—and I interviewed at about six or seven major corporations—I found a status quo that wanted me to file away my brain for a good dozen years before they'd ask my opinion.

I still laugh when I think about my interview with Proctor & Gamble. It was a laborious process of interviewing—one hour each with eight different people. Finally I sat down with the director of personnel. The first thing he asked was whether I wanted to be known as Kenneth, my real name, or Hap, a name I'd had since childhood. "Hap," I said. "That's what all my friends call me."

He looked at me for a moment, kind of tugged at his tie. Rubbed his chin. And with a deep authority in his voice that made me know he was making a serious, corporate-type decision, he said, "I think you'd be better off as Kenneth."

I bit my tongue and waited.

Then came his second question. "So, Kenneth, what's your vision of the future? If we were to hire you, what role would you play in the company in, say, five years?"

I looked at him. He was this sad little humanoid with a Mommy's-boy face and just enough authority to give him a bully's demeanor. I could imagine him in grade school getting thrown against his locker, pleading for his life and offering his lunch money for ransom. This moment, I assumed, was his revenge. "In five years," I said, "if I were to be here, and I underscore the word *if*, I would expect to be president. I guess that means passing you in five minutes, and that doesn't seem like any big deal to me."

Reverence to titled authority, as you can see, has never been one of my strong points. I believe respect must be earned, and I also believe the primary person you should respect is yourself. After my meeting with the personnel director at Proctor & Gamble, I felt good about myself. It was fun to tweak this functionary and his bullying ways. He hadn't earned my respect. He wouldn't even call me by the name I chose. I knew my own abilities, and I knew my life wouldn't end if the humanoid didn't like me.

The truth is, though, he did like me. Maybe not as a friend, but he saw deep enough to know I could help the company. Despite our rather pointed conversation, he offered me a job. I declined. A company that would give this man authority, I thought, is a maelstrom I would prefer not to enter.

I've seen it a thousand times in business—rejection of an idea or a person by virtue of corporate status. The powers that be have authority, so they must be right. Right? Sure, the world's flat too. What they have is the fraud of authority, the power to be a bully by the virtue of their title. A title, however, makes no one a leader.

It is usually easier to lead with a title than without. Leading without a title is one of the most difficult and courageous things anyone can attempt. Often, leaders without titles arise in the midst of a crisis—a crisis like a bully's ego trip.

Dealing with a bully is not especially complicated or difficult. It merely takes nerve. If you work for such a person, do not submit. Fight for your dignity. Bullies destroy dignity and they destroy companies. If you are a leader, you must not allow them to operate under you. As a leader you should try to reform the bully—attempt to make a human connection that explains why people deserve respect. If this does not work, then you must fire that person. Bullies set entirely the wrong tone for productivity, passion, and fun. They drain energy.

The funny thing about these tyrants is that when they lie or back stab or threaten, they think that no one else notices. The truth is, everyone notices because these things get around. And so the fraud of authority becomes transparent, a shameless ego trip. Employees obey, but they don't believe. How can they share the dream of a person they privately loathe? They can't.

Who are these monoliths—these institutional fascists wallowing in their muck of false glory? They come in all shapes and sizes. All colors and both sexes too, though in business they are usually white males. Inevitably what makes them a universal plague on the worker is their bald cruelty. Some do it like smiling assassins—lying to save face while turning the knife in your back. Others are more honest, but just as cruel—shouting you down like a verbal storm trooper. Either way, the mission is to destroy dreams. Dreams *and* dreamers.

Let me give you an example. Not that I need to; I know that if you have worked a length of time for an unenlightened employer, you know what I am saying. You can probably remember a specific example. I bet you can remember exact scenes, smells, words.

Allen Culver certainly can. Culver is a retail executive—a hired hand, if you will. Although he is not a career hopper, there is a bit of a hired-gun quality to him. He is the man you hire in the retail business if you want results. But this is no Clint Eastwood. He is a fun man, an ingratiating person—friendly and warm.

And so he was in 1984 when he was hired by a major retail drugstore chain headquartered in the Midwest. The company, which was in trouble, had been acquired three years earlier by an industrial conglomerate. It began to hide the problem of the drug chain's poor results inside the larger corporate finances of the parent company.

In two years the conglomerate had fired two presidents of the drug chain, and in 1984 it hired Allen Culver for that position. He was told he was taking over a very healthy company, and they showed him numbers to support that. But what they failed to tell him was that some of the numbers in the financials, such as cost of goods, were not reality but rather from a six-month-old budget. In other words, Culver was not told that the company had actually lost $6 million.

Over the next six months the truth began to trickle out. Actually, as much as anything, Culver rooted it out. He learned that the company was not healthy and had probably been made to appear healthy to attract someone like himself to run it. When Culver approached the leaders of the conglomerate for an explanation, he was told, "What's a little lie among friends?"

And then he was told, "It should take five years to turn the chain around." The CEO of the conglomerate gave Culver one of those supercilious John Wayne–CEO looks: the kind of look learned in third grade, refined in ninth grade, and put to use by every bully in America. "But that five-year period started two years ago. You've got three years to do it," he said. After all, he explained, "It's been two years since we bought the chain. So what if you were hired six months ago? You're working on the last guy's clock."

Culver was amazed. He couldn't believe he'd even agreed to work for these people. He couldn't believe how backhanded they were. People deserve honesty and respect, he told them. His argument fell on deaf ears.

The atmosphere repulsed him. He started noticing it everywhere, like a foul smell that grows until it is unbearable. He didn't understand the CEO's motivation, but he knew the atmosphere it created was not right for him or the company. He began looking for another job.

In retrospect, he probably should have seen what was coming in his first week. On his first day on the job he was greeted by a member of the public relations department, who said they needed his picture. Something about promotional materials. Typical PR bullshit, but necessary nevertheless. One of those little trade-offs you make for success.

Culver went in and they snapped his picture. "I'd like input in choosing the photo you use," he said. They agreed.

But then a week later a business journal came out with a story on Culver and his picture. It was a mean image—no smile, almost a scowl on his face. Unbeknownst to him, the company had done a full PR release on his hiring, including the meanest no-smiling photo of the lot.

Culver went to the CEO of the conglomerate. "I don't really like this image of myself. I'd like to put myself across as a bit more pleasant, as someone with an enlightened perspective," he said.

"I don't care what you want," said the CEO. "I want you to look tough."

From the beginning the relationship was a false one. Everything flowed in one direction. The CEO wouldn't listen. He didn't inspire. He dwelt on the negative. The argument over the picture was not just that it was the wrong image for Culver, but also that Culver's authority must not be co-opted by the parent company if it was to expect success. As a leader Culver knew he couldn't work within the false parameters set up by a man without empathy. Culver knew empathy between himself and the CEO required empathy in general from the CEO for the workers and their beliefs.

He gave it his best, but as stories like this often go, Culver and the conglomerate eventually parted company. It was a courteous parting, but the waste of a very talented man. The case is so typical, it's sad. Here is a man more than qualified to do a job. And he is a happy, creative, cheerful hard worker. This is a dream employee, but what is he faced with—muck. The muck of false glory spewed about by an ego-bound CEO.

The bully knows everything, of course, except how to let a human talent flourish. Instead he creates a muck—an embalming fluid for the soul, suffocating the employees. And the bully is like a grim mortician, pouring gobs of cake makeup onto the faces of the dead so that they are all lifeless clones of his image.

Only a few—the Allen Culvers of the world—dare to swim in this embalming fluid. It is indeed a complex, challenging mixture the fascists have fashioned.

The embalming fluid of business is no mere chemical concoction dreamed up by heartless analysts. It has a more sinister quality to it, a duplicity that works like black magic, rendering all who don't fight for their life to a fate of absolute apathy.

What Culver learned was that his company could not afford to let him do his job as he saw fit. They beat him down, or tried to at least, by declaring his way, his smile, his happiness to be nonproductive. They tried to break him.

The problem is respect. The bullies have no respect because, in many cases, they are not leaders. Some clearly have no talent. But many do; just no leadership talent. Classically they ride the system. They were *A* students all through school but wouldn't know the difference between a red light and a green one when it comes to street smarts.

They test well, but they live as if life were a series of exams instead of adventures.

They sit in their throne room of an office and look down on all employees. These people, lower on the corporate food chain, have been beaten down and thus, they cower—afraid even to wear the wrong color tie or wrong style shoes.

This weighted system is installed with fear and with rewards—it examines everything but talent and drive. *Who was your cousin? Did you go to Stanford? Do you have an MBA, and do you speak Flemish? Will you do everything we say without question?*

Susan Butcher knows all about this. Butcher is a native of Cambridge, Massachusetts—hometown of Harvard and the Eastern intellectual elite. A nice place, but not exactly the great outdoors for an adventurer.

Somehow Butcher found her way to Alaska and became interested in dog sledding. The interest gave way to obsession—it would define her. The sport became her life.

No sport in the world had been more of a man's domain than dog sledding. A man and his dogs. Alone. A gun by his side and a passion to his stare. The gun was to fend off polar bears, wolves, moose, and other dangerous animals. The stare was also a tool—a necessary gait in the attitude.

The pinnacle of dog sledding is the Iditarod Trail race, 1,150 miles of equally intense weather and scenery. It runs from Anchorage to Nome. The land is spectacular in its desolation. Shades of white on white, pale skies, and a gigantic silence. The challenges of the Iditarod change from year to year. The only constant is loneliness.

Usually, the weather is cold and crisp—the type that can freeze shut the eyes of a racer. Ice constantly forms in beards and eyebrows. Sometimes, however, the weather is warm and the snow is soft; then sleds and dogs break through the crust, making it impossible to ride. Racers often must run alongside the sled. Sometimes they have to pick up the sled and carry it over obstacles. A rider's dogs can be attacked by wild animals, or they can die of exhaustion. One year the race was held up by the migration of thousands of moose. Another year the fog became so dense that many mushers got lost.

Into this world of men, in the late 1970s, walked Susan Butcher. She wasn't even Alaskan.

People scoffed. She had entered the land of *Can't.* "You can't," she was told. "It's dangerous . . . You're a woman . . . We're only thinking about your safety."

The men were thinking about their egos. They may have had some genuine concern about her safety; that is felt for every racer. But their major concern was about jeopardizing the purity of their private club. This is for men, honey. Go home and sew something.

They had their little laughs while they toasted one another in their local bars. But Susan Butcher went on to win the Iditarod four times, the most times for anyone in the history of the race. In 1990 she was voted athlete of the year by *Sports Illustrated.*

Susan Butcher proved everyone wrong by sledding right around the embalming fluid of sexism. She entered the most intense dog race in the world—a race that almost bubbles over with opportunities for *can't*—and she won. And then she did it again. And again. And again.

Last year, Rick Swenson won his fifth, just beating out Susan. But she is still driven and intends to keep competing—and winning. They are still saying *can't*—No one, not a woman or even a man, can win the Iditarod six times. That's what they say.

But from the beginning we at The North Face recognized her talent. I am proud to say that we were the first company to sponsor her. We recognized and supported her quest and leadership long before it was topical, and long before she ever won an Iditarod race. Some of it was luck (she knocked on our door), and some of it was insight. When we sponsored someone, it was never just for business purposes. We took a special interest in people and their passions because we were genuinely interested.

The monoliths will always have you believe that you are in God's Little Waiting Room. You don't live; you wait under their control. Quiet resignation is their goal for you.

They do it in so many ways. Little ways that grow big. Big ways that can't be ignored.

Doors. They do it with doors—barriers that suggest you are not to come in; you are not good enough. They close the door to their office, and they put a gaudy brass nameplate on it that clearly says, "This person is *really* important."

They do it with labels—when they label things "executive," such as the executive washroom, or the executive dining room, or the executive parking space. What feudal crap! It's medieval, this tier system of privilege. It says you are nothing if you don't have access to these perquisites. If you listen to this, you might even start believing it. A company that loses touch with its employees loses everything.

As for an executive parking space, all I can say is, get to work early if you want a good parking space. It's that simple.

Electronic computer access is another barrier. You can't have information. There it is, *can't* again. Knowledge is power, and they don't want to give it away. This time you are not trusted. They dream up a secret password and then refuse to give it to you—limiting the access you have to vital information about the company. Often it is precisely the information you need for timely, accurate decision making. But so vital is this information, apparently, it is more vital than you.

That's how it always is, isn't it? The employee is the least-valuable part of the company. Just a cog in the wheel, right? Stick 'em in the embalming fluid of the workaday world and watch the body die.

Richard Bangs used to meet up with those people all the time. It was Ethiopia, 1973. The Omo river. It had never been run on a raft before.

Bangs set running the Omo as a personal goal, a life quest at age 22. So, like anyone serious who wants to accomplish anything, he began studying and asking questions about the nature of his goal. He went to zoos, museums, libraries, anywhere he could find out about the Omo River.

Everybody told him he was insane—too young and too inexperienced to even try. They told him about crocodiles and hippos, and poisonous snakes, and unpredictable diseases.

He had nightmares. His imagination ran wild. But he had been a river guide for the five years he attended Northwestern University. He had been a river guide on the mighty Colorado River, taking powerful clients such as the president of MGM, corporate lawyers, and even movie stars on the rides of their lives.

Of that time period Bangs told me, "It was incredible. I was in awe of them. If I went to their offices, I couldn't get inside the door. But on that raft, they relied on me." Those four sentences describe perfectly what I am trying to say: If leaders respect the skill and opinions of others, they have a lot to gain. And if they don't respect them, they are in grave danger.

Bangs thought he was in grave danger when he listened to the experts. He had never even undertaken an adventure outside the United States before. They were right, the trip *did* sound insane. But he never thought of cancelling it. He just dwelt on how to solve what might go wrong. Finally he hopped on a plane and flew to Ethiopia. He imagined the worst. And he prepared for it.

As soon as he arrived, he knew he was right. The dream was not impossible. The Omo River was doable, and his career as a writer, professional adventurer, and head of an adventure-travel company was launched.

The Omo River was intense. At one point a crocodile locked its jaws on the front of Bangs's inflatable raft and the three passengers had to row frantically for ten minutes until the croc finally let go.

But Richard Bangs, who has also published numerous books, was faced with his biggest challenge a few years later when circumstances led even him to say *can't.*

Up to then, he had had nothing but success. He named his adventure-travel company, Sobek, after the crocodile god that rules over the Omo River. The company provides some of the most exciting and exhilirating adventures for clients that you can imagine. By the mid-1970s Bangs was, as he said, "pushing the envelope further and further. I became too cocky."

He did it not only in the adventure world but also in the business world. For him, the two went hand in hand. Bangs helped organize a run of the Baro River, a major tributary of the White Nile in the rain forest of southwest Ethiopia. To help pay for the trip Bangs allowed a relative novice, although a superb athlete—a professional soccer player—to come on the trip. The lure of money was strong. The soccer player sold his sports car to come.

What happened in Ethiopia has haunted Bangs ever since. The raft they were in capsized, and the soccer player and Bangs were thrown off. Bangs initially saved the soccer player's life in the middle of the water by cutting the boat's stern line, which had wrapped itself around the sports star's body. Bangs did this while floating and bouncing through the river with him.

"Swim for shore!" Bangs yelled. The soccer player nodded, and Bangs headed off to try to rescue the raft. That was the last time anyone saw the young soccer player. Bangs had his own close call as he bounced, unprotected, through the rapids.

When Bangs regained consciousness after blacking out on the side of the river, he and the others began searching. Ten days later they gave up. The soccer player's body was never found.

Bangs gave up adventuring completely. He went to graduate school and received a degree in journalism. Whenever he saw his friends from the adventuring world, he told them they were crazy. He told them of the dangers.

This would be a very sad story if it weren't for one thing: the inner fortitude of Richard Bangs. He could only stay away from the world's great adventures for so long. Eventually he was seduced back to his true love—life as an adventurer.

Bangs has a theory about all this, and he incorporates it into his business, which today is called Mountain Travel/ Sobek. "As I examined it, life without risk is a passionless life—a life not worth living," he told me. "You know, everybody is capable of pushing themselves beyond inner perceived limits. If they can just take that first step, whole new worlds open up. An enormous number of people say at first they wouldn't take an adventure vacation. It's just not part of their personality. But when they do take a trip, you can watch them blossom. They become overpowered by positive feelings. When they come back from an adventure, they apply these changes to their lives."

When whole new worlds open up, life becomes fun again. Joy has overwhelming power. When joy is a by-product of work, limits disappear.

American business has overlooked the power of fun in relation to productivity. Fun exists as a product (for example, in the entertainment business) but not as a tool. It is just another example of how the embalming fluid has soaked into the fabric of most businesses. Fun is discouraged. The implication is that if fun is allowed, work becomes secondary. I challenge that. I know better. If fun and effort are related, success in an open company comes naturally.

During a recent economic downturn in the retail market Levi Strauss, a fine company, unwittingly put their employees in embalming fluid. The company had built a wonderful new facility with beautiful terraces used for coffee areas and lounges. It would be great for employees to unwind on the terraces—tell a joke, laugh a little, refuel emotionally and mentally.

But when the market turned down and people had to be laid off, Levi found people were afraid to go into these areas. They did not want to appear to be loafing or having fun. They did not want to endanger their jobs. So the terraces—built to say to employees, we care—stood empty, like a museum piece from a long-ago age of compassion and good economic times.

Levi solved the problem. They put common work areas, for example those with duplicating machines and postage meters, in these areas so employees could enjoy the space without guilt. Levi tried to incorporate joy into production. It was a step in the right direction.

It still didn't solve the problem of why people felt guilty about taking a break, but at least it allowed them to enjoy the new building.

At The North Face, the company I started in 1968 and built into the industry leader for outdoor equipment, our growth gave us a space problem too. At the time our company was about eight years old, and we needed to fit more employees into our building.

We knew from industry studies that our sewing-machine operators could work in less space—28 square feet instead of 36 square feet. However, we had been successful because of our loyalty to our workers and because we made their working conditions as comfortable as possible. Each employee had his or her own "territory," and we didn't want to disturb that. But we needed the space if we were going to grow. And we were going to grow; no question about that.

We didn't want to just take away their space—that would have been demoralizing. Instead, we were honest. We said, look, we have this problem. We want to grow, and we know we can. It will be good for all of us, but we know that if we do, it will require that we take something away from you, some of the space around your machine. It's not our first choice, but under the circumstances it's the best choice.

We then offered something back. It was not the greatest gift an employee ever received. But they knew it came from our hearts, so they accepted it. It was their own personalized nameplate for their work space. Something that identified a part of the company as their very own. Our message was clear: You, the employee, matter. Without you, we could not have had the success we have, and we wouldn't be able to continue our spectacular growth. By the way, none of our executives ever had their name on their door or desk.

We took two weeks to explain this, individually, to each production worker. Every one accepted the offer. They had something most production workers never have—pride, identity, and respect.

The embalming fluid of business can be so many different things. At Levi and The North Face it was as simple as building design. The answer is, as it always is, honesty and compassion coupled with a dash of creativity. Explain the problem; show you care.

Too many companies do not care. They expect employees to have a Muzak personality, and they run their companies with absolutely no verve.

Too many employees let themselves get beaten down—they give in to the monarchs in their mahogany castles. They don't have a let's-do-something-right attitude. Instead, the attitude is, I won't piss anyone off. In most companies the employee motto is Cover Thy Butt. If you examine where that attitude originated, inevitably you will find it is also the motto of the executives.

Once I ran into a flood of embalming fluid like I'd never seen before. It was 1975. I had been invited by a couple of outside directors to New York for a special board meeting of The North Face.

Our company had always operated on a foundation of exuberance and vibrance. Quality was our forte—we prided ourselves on being the best. We had become the industry leader through product innovation. Our investment was in market dominance for the long term. It was fun to walk the high wire, but there was no pretense in anyone.

The meeting was held in the University Club, a pretentious mid-Manhattan monument to the Ivy League. The hanging chandeliers sparkled onto the hand-carved mahogany walls, which rose majestically 20 feet from floor to ceiling. It was a hard place for delicate emotions. The curtains were thick velvet and blocked off all light and noise from the outside world. Antiseptic.

At the University Club, toying with companies was entertainment. Walking into the garish confines, one had to fight the feeling of being a pawn in someone else's power game. These board members didn't care about people or quality, only image and control. Their decisions were made totally out of the context of reality. Issues like leadership, humanism, commitment, and vision were ignored. It was our lives, but they didn't care. The only thing that mattered was the game, where winning and losing are merely words.

I was invited to attend my own firing by a group of dissident board members. They didn't put it that way, but we both knew why they had called the meeting. They felt the company had outgrown me, that I was an entrepreneur in a company that called for management. It is a common, and mistaken, venture capitalist assumption that all entrepreneurs are unable to run companies once they grow. They had their MBAs. I had my MBA. They had the money. I had something better—a highly successful company.

Four of us entered together. We were an hour late when we walked through the marbled entrance and took the elevator to the top floor. We had been trying to work out an agreement to restructure the management of the company, but we couldn't. Basically, I had refused. They wanted to push me aside and eliminate the leadership, replacing me with a manager who would acquiesce to their demands. It was our company, everybody's company, and I wouldn't sell out. Thus high drama at the University Club. What a joke this was—I still laugh about it with my friends. Here we were, a relatively small company operating on an austere budget, spending thousands just to rent the room only to satisfy the tastes and whims of a few board members. While they talked about results, they didn't have a clue as to the forced discipline it took to get results. They were spending more for that one get-together than our office supplies bill was for an entire month.

The room was ridiculous. It was totally out of context for a company that made mountaineering, backpacking, and other wilderness equipment. It wasn't even one room; it was three. There was a cocktail room with two bars and servants. The second room was the board room, with high-backed leather chairs and a Caucasian testosterone ooze. This was an old boys' club. The third room, the most elaborate of them all, was for lunch.

There I was, the iconoclast. They were the icons. In all there were 12 of us at the meeting, including my management. The junior board members preened and postured for their elders. The senior members did the power-word thing, and I must say they were quite good at it. They'd dance and balance jugular tendencies with parliamentary etiquette. It was most impressive. They had become masters at doing something of zero benefit to society. They were diplomatic bullies.

The chairman of the board and I entered. We explained why we were late, and the game began. I knew it was mine to lose, and I saw that it could slip away very fast. Rather than delay, I invited confrontation.

My format was simple. I would be honest. "Yes, this year's earnings forecast was not met," I said. "But the North Face was the largest and best in the industry, and one of the best small businesses in the country." There was plenty of documented evidence to prove this. I explained that one problem was the use of aggressive forecasting to motivate employees. The other problem was that we had made a bad hire in the finance department. The individual we had hired failed to set up adequate systems to give us operational control of our inventories. Thus the numbers he reported were inaccurate. When we took physical inventories, there was significant shortfall from his reported members.

"We replaced that person," I said. "Progress is now excellent." I pointed out to the board that the company had grown dramatically in the preceding year in both sales and earnings.

"I have a proposal," I said. "Give the remaining management six months to prove that we can, with this one personnel change, not only continue our dramatic growth but also reach our forecasts. The same forecasts. Just give me six months. If we can't, my entire management will resign without argument."

They were silent. I assumed they had already made up their minds. But I pressed on. If I was going out, I was going out honestly. The chairman finally spoke. He was complimentary. He spoke of my talent, my vision. It was too much. And then slowly, skillfully, he turned the corner. A dual head to the company, he proposed.

Take it or leave. That was the proposal. Take the offer of someone to, in effect, watch over me, or leave the company. Not exactly those words. He veiled it in semantics, but his intent was clear. The chairman smiled at me and then went to work on the board.

"A rejection of this proposal would be divisive to the board," said the chairman. "It could perhaps split it irreparably and lead to the demise of The North Face. If that happened, it would all be on Hap's shoulders."

It was curious to hear the chairman say my name as if

he were my friend. If it hadn't been for the pressure of the situation, I would've laughed. "We shouldn't let Hap risk his wealth when the problem could easily be solved by Hap acceding to this proposal." There was such sincerity in his voice. What a phony. He sat there wearing a red sash from his shoulder to his hip like some foreign dignitary. It was absurd.

I felt like a street fighter who had walked into an ambush. But instead of a dark alley, I was in the midst of leather and velvet. "I won't accept your proposal," I said. I felt a lump in my throat. This was my life. My body filled with adrenaline. My eyeballs became huge as the whole scene clarified. "If you want to fire me, go ahead." I remember those words. I can still taste them. They weren't bitter; they were survivalistic. "But I know and you know," I said, "that you are wrong!"

I needed those in that room to understand the passion that ran through my company—the commitment I had asked of and received from my employees. I of course knew it was more complex than that. But I had to get them to understand that our company wouldn't submit to being a faceless pawn on their game board. They needed to know this was about people.

It worked. They backpedaled. "I don't think we should walk headlong into these important decisions," said the chairman, after a long pause. He suggested lunch and cocktails.

We went to the next room. But even though the meeting later continued, the confrontation was over. I had stood up to them. I had swum through their foul embalming fluid and lived to write about it. Six months later The North Face had more than met our forecasts. Our board room solution had been to bring in a consultant to analyze the company and report back to the board. Six months later the consultant gave his report. He said the company was being run very well—as well as he could imagine it being run. And 15 years later, in 1989, I sold the company for $5.4 million. The company's sales at the time I sold it had increased tenfold from those on the day of the meeting. It was a profound change indeed.

To leaders, I say lead. Nurture talent; it is your best resource. To employees, I say stay strong, act out, contribute. And to all who work in America, I say don't just let it all be. Do something. Don't just let global competitors win. Take risks and smile. Have some fun—it's not against the rules. At least it shouldn't be. If you do nothing, nothing happens. If you don't swim through the embalming fluid, you drown.

As Richard Bangs once told me when talking about the expeditions he leads, "The longer somebody is out there and the more difficult the challenge, the greater the probability that person will profoundly change." The same is true in business.

If you want to know if an employer is drowning its employees in embalming fluid, just walk into the work area and see if anyone looks at you. See if they take their eyes off their work for even one moment to greet you, to smile at you, to show they are alive. If they do not, the leadership has beaten them down. If the rules are set up to suck the life from employees, it inevitably will do so from all but the most determined. And those most determined will never stick around to help the company. They will cut their own swath—determined to prove business does not have to be lifeless.

2

Digging Below the Bottom Line:

The Numbers Don't Tell the Story

"Doing things the old way," Steve Powell told the *Wall Street Journal* in 1991, "is like trying to clap with one hand."

Powell is senior adviser on human resources at British Petroleum Exploration—the arm of BPE that is most dependent on creativity. British Petroleum has set out to reduce the layers of management and thus clap with both hands. Sure, logic suggests you should try to reduce bureaucracy. But BPE has a deeper reason for doing this, one much closer to the core of the decision. The company is going to reward ingenuity and talent instead of ladder climbing. The

Wall Street Journal said this shift in philosophy "could turn out to be a revolution in corporate culture, with far-reaching applications in other industries' . . . and the changes at BP Exploration will fundamentally alter the way the company is run."

"Fundamentally alter." "Revolution." Big words. And you know what—the folks at the *Journal* are right. Although they hid those words in a 15-paragraph column called "International Manager," they used all the right words. This is a tremendous idea.

In essence it would overhaul the way employees are evaluated, promoted, and compensated. It would reward creativity without forcing people into management.

Imagine getting rewarded for staying in your job and performing well. You don't have to move up into a job you don't want. There is a better way to make good money and receive recognition. You simply have to do a good job and keep getting better. You are measured on how good you are, not on how many meetings you attend. It's staggering.

Let's think about bowling balls. Brunswick is the largest American company that makes bowling balls. A few years back Brunswick had a dilemma. Their product was better than their warehouse equipment.

Bowling balls weigh between nine and 19 pounds each and so are quite heavy when sent out in bulk. Brunswick had a huge warehouse. The problem was the overhead equipment used to move inventory. The bearings in this equipment kept breaking down. It was a simple problem, but the solution was expensive.

Brunswick replaced the bearings. The bearings broke. Again and again. They kept breaking. Brunswick put their engineers on the problem. The engineers tried and tried to design unbreakable bearings, but to no avail. Finally some warehouse workers had an idea. Brunswick, to its credit, listened.

The workers suggested an inexpensive, ingenious, commonsense solution. Each month, they pointed out, bowling balls were returned to Brunswick because they had minor flaws—usually something to do with color.

Why not redesign the machines a bit so that they could use the rejects as bearings? suggested the workers. Then, even if they break down, they are cheap to replace.

My favorite part of this story comes next. A few months later representatives of the Japanese company that was Brunswick's partner visited the United States. The Japanese saw the new bearings and were impressed by the ingenuity of the Americans.

However, something was definitely lost in the translation. A few months later when the Americans went to Japan, they found the Japanese using the same system, with one variation. Instead of rejected balls, the Japanese were using new bowling balls. Factory made, right there. And, incredibly, they had even taken the time to drill the three finger holes into each ball. That way, explained the Japanese, they are exactly like those used in the United States.

Apparently the Japanese never realized the holes were only in U.S. bearings because Brunswick was using recycled product. The Japanese didn't take the time to measure anything but the financial success of this approach. The American company was successful because it used bowling balls as its bearings. And, thought the Japanese, it's cheaper to make bowling balls than to buy designer bearings. They didn't look any further than the bottom line to understand the total ingenuity of the solution.

It is unusual for a Japanese company not to look below the bottom line. Unfortunately it is all too common for an

American company. No matter what the company, though, it is essential to expand the number of measurements you use to determine its health. Too many companies are being run by professional, MBA-type managers. Many are water bugs skimming over the waters of commerce, more intent on their own career paths than on learning about the intricacies of their business or the passions of their people.

Just as blood pressure and heart rate tell only part of the story in relation to the health of a human body, so too do profits tell only part of the story about any company. Unfortunately many executives are trained to hear "get your profits up" to mean the same as "get your blood pressure down." The thinking is that if you do, everything else will fall into place.

It sure is simple. One goal—short-term profits. But life is not that way. Business certainly is not that way. Although you need to simplify, not complicate, your goals, you must also realize there are a vast number of opportunities to both measure and improve your company. There are new ways to look at things, fresh perspectives. But you have to get beyond blood pressure and heart rate. You have to somehow measure the soul of your company.

The Japanese bowling ball company, for instance, never took the time to measure employee satisfaction at Brunswick. They never noticed, as they entered the Brunswick factory, that the employees were smiling, happy to meet them, and proud of their own work. Instead they looked at the bearings with the three finger holes.

They never even looked, really, at the bowling balls. They never stopped to think why the balls were better than the bearings. Oh, sure, they thought about the cost involved—the bottom line. If they had looked at the bowling balls on another level, they would have realized that drilling the holes was a waste of time and money. And if they had examined that aspect further, they would have understood just what the Americans were up to—recycling unwanted stock. But no; they saw only money.

Narrowing every business analysis to profit and loss would be like a ski area narrowing its focus to just its hills. The Vail Associates, Inc., under the leadership of George Gillette, looked far beyond the hills into what was essential for a great skiing business—humanity. Vail is dedicated to quality and consumer satisfaction. All Vail employees are trained to enhance the customer's vacation. The training includes a study of customer psychology and ways to satisfy the customer.

Gillette had a vision to make his a new type of ski resort—not just a spectacular destination, but a family destination as well. Home in the Rockies. He and his team wanted it to be a place families would talk about 12 months a year. They wanted Vail to be not just a destination, but *the* destination.

They wanted children to talk about it. It had to be extraordinary, and it was. They had more than hot chocolate, one instructor, and a day-care center. They thought it through and imagined what it would be like to be a child on vacation on a mountain.

They put up teepees. They made a ski run go right through an Old West fort, with 20-foot-high sentry towers on either side of the run. Arrows are embedded in the fort. Vail humanized the experience and connected to the curiosity of every child. Best of all, they connected to the concept of letting children be children. No adults, except for instructors, are allowed on the run.

Business is about so many things, it is foolish and inaccurate to narrow down success to profit and loss. It is the same with people. A sparkling resume may be a good indicator of someone's potential, but it may not. There are always other things to consider.

One of the most intelligent employees I ever hired at The North Face was a single mother of three living on food stamps, welfare, and her wits. Her resume was not exactly sparkling, but I took the time to look beyond her lack of employment.

I was impressed, you see, because she had figured out how to beat the system—definitely my type of employee. She had an "old man" who was the father of one of her children. They didn't get married because it would cut the payments in half, and he claimed to live elsewhere for the same reason.

To get money to pay the rent, she baby-sat other children along with her own for income that she didn't have to report. At night, when her old man was around, she worked in the garden of a local vegetable producer and was paid in vegetables and other food.

And she sold small amounts of marijuana that she grew in her apartment. The fact that she sold marijuana didn't thrill me, but I learned long ago that it is not what people are but rather who they are that counts. The reason I got a lot of great employees was that I took the time to look at who they were—I got to know them. I know circumstances dictate a lot of what people do in life. It is how they overcome those circumstances that identifies the difference between good employees and great employees. I look for the latter.

The way I met her was that she and a friend, using the friend's truck, used to pick up scraps from our factory in Berkeley. She used scrap fabrics and filling from The North Face to make stuffed toys for children, and she also picked the trash at other Berkeley factories to make other toys, like marbles from glass beads. After she made the toys, she baby-sat for her friend's children while the friend sold the toys at flea markets.

Finally she had enough money to buy a car and pay for a baby-sitter. I was so impressed with her background, I hired her. At The North Face she had a real job making constant money and she had health benefits. And better yet, for our company, she increased our can-do attitude. She was a seamstress who ended up working in our warranty department. She was excellent. When people came in, they liked dealing with her, and it reflected well on The North Face. I am convinced it was because her various experiences and positive attitude enabled her to identify with those who came in needing repairs.

The truth is, in life as in business the numbers often don't tell the story. In the earliest days of business everything was based on the agrarian calendar. Harvest-time was the ultimate measuring stick. This yearly measure made perfect sense when sustenance was the goal. But times have changed, and a yearly measuring stick of profits, though important, should not be the end-all.

No one fact standing alone means much of anything. Just as the mere fact of a mother being on welfare does not make her ignorant, so it is with money. Profits, especially short-term profits, do not equal success. Profits are to be factored in, certainly. But the goals of a business are now more complex than a quarter-to-quarter, year-to-year measurement of an increase in profits. A truly successful company is one that inspires its employees, one with a true sense of its role in the marketplace, and one with far-reaching goals that look beyond the bottom line at the end of the next quarter toward long-term prosperity.

Adventuring, like business, is not just about who goes

the highest or the farthest. The highest mountains have already been climbed. Adventuring means doing things in different ways—measuring one's self within the parameters of individuality. Sir Ranulf Fiennes decided his quest was walking around the globe. Steve McKinney chose to hang glide off Mt. Everest. Numerous people parapent (use highly guidable parachutes) off mountains. Jan Reynolds became the first person (and woman) to balloon over Everest. Rheinhold Messner climbs without partners or oxygen. Everyone defines adventure and success on his or her own terms. In fact, one of the happier people I've met is a man who became a butterfly rancher in Guatemala.

Another satisfied adventurer is Royal Robbins, who learned through the mistakes of others how to look at the big picture. The first thing you notice about Royal is his eyes, because they are intense, intelligent, twinkling. His are active eyes, the kind that always say, "What's that?" in sincere curiosity.

Royal is a gentle man, not large in stature, but strong and smart enough to get a well-earned reputation as one of the best rock climbers in the history of Yosemite National Park. And he is funny. There is something splendid about his sense of humor, his way of making you laugh at situations you could never imagine. His humor is like his eyes, very engaging. A connection comes easily with Royal.

And so it was when he told me about Dru Mountain in Switzerland. Some had succeeded in climbing it, but many had failed. Most of the climbers had years of experience and months of training. They had the skill, equipment, and desire necessary to climb most mountains. But for the Dru, something else was needed. Most of the failures had resulted from becoming caught midclimb in the volatile weather. Driving rain or snow had pushed them back.

Royal smiled at this next part. "The problem," he said, "was that no one took the time to examine the weather patterns. It was really quite easy once I thought about it."

The weather, though volatile, went in a predictable cycle. So Royal did the opposite of everyone else—he started his climb in bad weather. He figured nature would swing back to good weather in time for the main assault. He was right.

His is an analytical approach. If such an approach is coupled with a healthy dose of passion, it is by far the best approach. Royal Robbins has the proper passion. Though he can seem pondering, he is anything but dull. Rather he is driven—a man in search of truth. He is not bullheaded in the sense of blind ambition. He is logical. When logic leads him to a solution, he is virtually unstoppable in his quest.

What Royal did was take the time to measure more than just the goal, the peak. He measured an obstacle, the weather, and then thought his way around it.

He didn't just measure profit. He measured all the things that stood in the way of profit, and all the things that helped him get profit. And although his problem didn't deal with humanity—it dealt with a living organism, the weather—he understood it. He could feel it, smell it, taste it, almost absorb it. He was in tune, and he knew what was happening—although he also knew that the weather, like anything with energy and a will, could change in an instant.

It is the same in business. Profit is one measurement, but so much goes into that one measurement. There is the energy level of the employees, satisfaction of customers, and creativity. Can these be measured? I say yes. Measured in terms of humanity.

An open mind can measure anything. You may not be able to quantify it, but you can measure it. Often it is an instinctual measurement—a singular, honest answer to your own questions. Are my employees giving me all they have? Do they have a reason to put forth such effort? Am I delivering the best possible product to my customers? Are we creative, or do we spurn creativity?

There is another point to be made here about quantifying these things. Profit itself is never accurately quantified. At least not in the short term—which is another reason to move beyond a quarter-to-quarter mentality. Profit can always be toyed with by a creative bookkeeper. You can set up or reduce reserves. You can come up with another acquisition and write things off under restructuring costs. You can roll profit over into another accounting period, choose different depreciation rates, and defer or accelerate payments or shipments. You can do so many things, legally, to alter short-term profit that it is really nothing more than a blood pressure test for the business.

Sure, profit means something. It is a guide, a barometer, but not a complete diagnostic measurement. Profit is not a bad measure; it is simply insufficient. It must be examined in conjunction with other factors. The thing about a measurement is that such a figure is not grounded without more information. It is merely a number up in the air. To say profit was $20 million means nothing. Profit on what, IBM or Joe's Hot Dog Stand?

There is an equation that goes into success, and you can reach the right answer in more than one way. Of course, the same is true for reaching the wrong answer. But one thing is constant. The most important part of the equation is humanity.

What most leaders do not understand is that profits are not just for the people at the top of the company. In many companies there are bonuses and stock options for a wide range of employees. People's whole lives are riding on the success of the company. Not just a few bucks—lives!

Let me give you an example of a factor that leads to profits that is both quantifiable and instinctual: energy level/satisfaction of employees. The easiest measure of this is employee turnover. Zero turnover is bad—it indicates complacency and acceptance of the status quo. High turnover is also bad. It is a sign of disgruntled employees. Turnover should not be a short-term measurement. It should be continuously monitored for trends, and corrective action should be taken when problems arise.

For a long time Sharper Image was considered a great business because of its rapid growth and profitability. But insiders knew better. They were measuring something else—employee satisfaction. What they saw, quite simply, was a turnover in excess of 100 percent a year. That's right, in excess of 100 percent. In other words, someone would quit, someone else would be hired, and then that person would quit all in the same year. More than 100 percent—incredible. People obviously found working for the company quite difficult. The owner was driving, demanding, intimidating, and never gave employees credit for their efforts. Suppliers were squeezed for advertising dollars. If they didn't spend more, the product was dropped. Quality was not as important as profits. The owner apparently would listen to no one, and employees couldn't leave fast enough. The owner didn't care—he was measuring profits.

In 1991, Sharper Image announced major financial and sales problems. The company said it must revamp its product focus and the internal workings of the company. Their latest plan is an environmental focus—claiming that as a company they want to get more in harmony with the world. Perhaps, but it might be better to concentrate on employee satisfaction because they're the ones who will make the sales increase.

One unquantifiable measure of employee satisfaction is employee comraderie—whether people care about one another and their jobs. It is tough to measure, but you can see it. If workers get together spontaneously, it is a good sign. They like one another. If get-togethers are farther and farther apart, a problem is brewing.

At a good company, birthdays are celebrated in some fashion. In a small company the entire company can celebrate. As a company grows, divisions can celebrate birthdays. The important thing is the human touch—such celebrations should be encouraged, even if the entire company cannot attend. In addition the anniversary of the company should be celebrated, as should new facilities or major achievements. At The North Face we always celebrated the company's anniversary. If these opportunities are ignored, the team is drifting apart.

Creativity is also something both measurable and abstract. Creativity is not something that should just be delegated to the design department. The warehouse workers at Brunswick proved that. Probably the easiest way to measure creativity is by examining the output of the design department—new products. Executives at 3M have told me that 80 percent of that company's products were created in the previous three years. Innovation is a constant goal for the company. Concepts such as quality and innovation cannot, however, be measured in just one department. They must be measured throughout the entire company.

An easy way to measure the output of the design department is to keep a running log of the research-and-development budget and compare it to profits for new products. If you keep these statistics for a three-year period, charting them on a graph makes it simple to spot trends. This may require a shift in your accounting to Activity-Based Accounting, but it will be worth it. In most businesses, R&D investments should show a return within that three years. However, in some businesses, such as the drug industry, the wait is much longer—for example the seven-year waiting period necessary for a new drug to be approved by the Food and Drug Administration. The parameters for a drug company are much different than for most other companies. You need to analyze and agree on the appropriate measures for your firm.

But creativity, of course, is more than R&D—it is a response to a company policy of listening, caring. No matter what the title of the employee—from janitor to senior researcher—each employee knows some aspects of the company better than top management.

One of the employees in 3M's adhesives division was also a singer in his church choir. He could never get the pieces of paper he marked hymns with to stay in his hymn book. They kept falling out. He suggested to 3M that a piece of paper with a light adhesive might be attractive to a few people. As it turned out, Post-Its were quite attractive to a lot of people.

Although you cannot quantify that type of creativity within a company, you can gauge it. Are employees coming to you with new ideas, even bad ones? Or have they been beaten down to the point that they no longer care? Are they drowning in embalming fluid, or are they flourishing in freedom?

There are, of course, other, more practical ways to measure success. Service is one easy way—turnaround time of orders in house. L. L. Bean, the mail-order house in Maine, does this. The company constantly measures not only its own turnaround time but also that of its competitors. Compensation and promotion within L. L. Bean are based in large part on service and turnaround time, and there is hell to pay if they start to slip.

What I am proposing is an expanded definition of success; something that incorporates a multitude of parameters into an always-fluid image of the company. This image is not only in the executive's mind. It is also, and more importantly, in the minds of the employees. It will include things I've talked about and things each individual dreams up. A good company can stand up to all fair standards. Perhaps the best standard is quality, which I will address in Chapter 9.

There are many little measurements that when plugged into the equation can lead to your analysis on the relative health and happiness of your company. One concrete measurement is market share. Japanese companies frequently approach the world with dominant market share as their goal. One such company is YKK, a zipper manufacturer. In the late 1960s YKK came to the United States with one goal—dominant market share. By 1970 they had only a negligible share of the market. They didn't panic—they remained focused on the long-term goal. Today YKK is the top company in the U.S. zipper market. They were flexible on pricing, hiring, and even location of their facilities. Instead of locating in a major, high-cost manufacturing center they went to Macon, Georgia. This allowed YKK to pump more money into customer service—they set up 20 service centers across the United States. It did not surprise me when I read in *Forbes* that the Yoshida family, which owns YKK, is one of the wealthiest families in the world.

Jack Akers, chairman of IBM, raised a major flap about market share in the spring of 1991: "The fact that we're losing market share makes me goddamn mad. . . . The tension level is not high enough; the business is in crisis." Those words appeared on the cover—yes, the cover—of *BusinessWeek* magazine.

In IBM's case, it seems, there is more to the problem than market share. Market share, like most things easy to measure, is a symptom. If market share is good, then the company is healthy. But if market share is bad or getting worse, you need to look for the disease. That can be deeply rooted and a bit harder to diagnose than simply health.

Another measure is Speed To Market. Entire businesses have been built on the premise of faster speed to market. Federal Express is an obvious one—proving time to be the commodity. Another is McDonald's. A classic is Revlon. Charles Revlon said, "To hell with R&D." His idea was to monitor the competitor's regional test-market ideas and then copy the good ones, reaching the entire market before the originator. Even though Revlon didn't invent many of its products, it often dominated the competition because it was faster at getting the products to market.

The Limited retail stores also have recognized the importance of Speed To Market. That company owns a fleet of private jets for the express purpose of flying new products from the Far East while the fashion is still hot. Their competitors rely on commercial shipping lines and lag.

Two more speed-to-market stores: Pillsbury and Ford. In 1988 Grand Metropolitan PLC acquired Pillsbury and sent in a small guerrilla team headed by Ian Martin to speed up Pillsbury. Martin is a no-nonsense Scotsman. He did away with the lethargic culture in the company. He eliminated layers of bureaucracy and reduced the product line. More important, he shortened the product incubation schedule by years. Profits went way up. Coincidentally Ford did the same thing after falling into deep trouble in the mid-

1980s. But when profits returned in the late 1980s, Ford fell back into its old lethargic ways—celebrating once again the committee. Rather than continue to try to improve, Ford stayed the same while its more aggressive foreign competition was always improving. In crisis, Ford focused. In success, it formed committees.

This is an example of a false summit, something very familiar to a mountaineer. Imagine being on a mountain. The struggle of the climb, the effort, the pain. All along you see what you think is the peak. You figure you have just enough energy to make it and when you do, man, it sure will feel great. Well, what often happens is when you reach the "peak" you realize it is only a step on the way to the real peak, which you see farther away. It is then that the mountaineer must really dig deep. A false summit can be tremendously demoralizing.

In business, reaching a goal can be like a false summit. Although the goal is real, it is important to immediately begin looking beyond the goal. A leader cannot steal away the joy employees feel for having reached the peak. But the leader also cannot let the energy level dissipate. It is very easy for everyone to fall into a sort of postpartum depression. In climbing, I have met very few climbers who do not describe a tremendously depressed feeling coming down from a successful climb. It is the feeling of "Is that all there is?"

At least in business, that is not all there is—goals continually evolve. To dig below the bottom line is to continually reach higher. Certainly it is important to set attainable goals so that business does not become a never-ending struggle to achieve the impossible. However, setting new goals is the only way to keep a company vibrant. In mountaineering being at the peak is only a small part of the joy. It is the actual struggle to get there that makes it fun.

Measuring success is not simple. Factoring in all the aspects of a company is the only true way to know its soul. After all, profits are temporal, but a soul—if it is strong—can live virtually forever.

And the bond that holds the soul of a company together is the people who work for it. Once the measuring is done, it must be constantly fed back to the employees so that they know where they stand and what to expect. I saw one of my clients try this and fail because he used so much business jargon and babble that he lost everyone in the linguistics. Business communication isn't some scientific formula—it is the same as any other communication. People must understand.

It's really that simple. When you read the numbers right, the thing you see is that every one of them represents a person or some people. They may work for you or for your competitor, be a supplier or be a customer. But they are there. Every number has a face.

3

FINDING THE SPARK:

Where Logic Meets Religion

The North Face was founded on what I call "the Scotch Principle." In Berkeley, 1968, scotch was not the usual principle, if you know what I mean. A group of us were sitting around having a 60s discussion about what turned out to be a very 80s discipline: making money. We were talking of what would become of us. "Imagine"—one person laughed—"where you'll be in ten years."

"Hap Klopp, more than thirty years old. That's a scary thought," said another.

But it wasn't. Not at all, and the scotch bottle started

making the rounds. "What the hell," someone offered after emptying his glass again. "Let's start a business."

"A business?" Another laughed. "What do we know? All we know is sports, outdoors, and having fun."

Not long afterward I bought three stores with a great image but severe financial problems that were called The North Face. I closed two of them and set out to design, produce, and market outdoor gear for the best adventures in the world.

Scotch. A bottle of scotch in 1968 in Berkeley, California, and my world changed completely. I am still in awe of how my company was dreamed up—except when I analyze it. On first glance, it seems against the American ethic to come up with a good idea in an intoxicated state. Just say no, right?

Well, I said yes. I am not here to advocate drunkenness, but rather to talk about leadership, personal freedom, and creativity. It always amazes me when I think of America as a place where I can go to a store and buy a machine gun, but I cannot legally buy one marijuana cigarette. I bet more good ideas have arisen in people after smoking a joint than anyone has ever had from shooting a hundred rounds a minute at a deer.

Nevertheless, there are many means to an end, and if yours happens to be squeezing the trigger of an AK-47, I say more power to you—as long as you don't harm anyone. Despite my disagreement with your means, I still believe you are among the lucky ones. If you have found a way to tap into yourself, your wants and your dreams, you should hold on to that with everything you have. Life is short, after all.

The world is changing at an ever-increasing pace. As a result, every day, every hour, sometimes every minute you need another new idea. Obviously you can't be wasted or shooting a machine gun all that time and be coming up with those ideas. Really, you can't even pretend to be anything but a jerk. Still, you've got to loosen up enough to listen to yourself because the real you holds the key to everything. You have to trust your instincts and then learn on an instant, personal basis. You must be free within yourself. To be aware of this skill and to tap into it at will can be an incredibly strong feeling—even a religious experience.

Nothing happens without a vision—the mental sweat of a single human spark. Get it where you will, but get it! Live to the fullest, trust yourself, and be honest. Don't *settle* for anything.

I remember reading an interview with a rock star. I don't remember the name of the performer, but I can picture the words as I can picture the faces of my children. He was talking about his struggles to make it and the "advice" he'd received from both friends and family. The guitar is great, they'd told him, but why don't you take up something else? Like welding or carpentry. Go to college—something. Just in case, they'd said. You know, so you have something to fall back on.

His response was simple. "If you have something to fall back on, you will fall back."

And so there is a spark. The world explodes like an orgasm hanging from a dream, and there is life—a compendium of opportunity from the seeds of an idea. This spark is where an active imagination meets hard work—where religion meets logic, and where God lives in all of us. I am not religious in a Jimmy-Swaggart-organized way, but I am religious in the sense that I cannot look at the ocean or mountains without thinking of God's majesty. And "spiritual" is the best word I can find to describe the spark. It is an inner dance of freedom that first admits and then proclaims, "I am this."

Generally vision comes from an inner need: emotional, psychological, or financial.

One spark. The Kockleman brothers have that spark, and what a spark it is. They are the incredible bungee brothers—real-life siblings who lead real-life bungee-cord adventures for profit. Bungee-cord jumping is the sport where you jump off a bridge with an elastic cord tied to both the bridge and your legs. The idea is to free-fall until almost hitting bottom and then be snatched from the jaws of death by the cord, which stretches but does not break.

Before the spark the Kocklemans were seemingly average Americans. Peter, the older, was an engineer. John was a computer consultant. But the two had always wanted to start a business together.

Theirs was not so much a spark as a lightning bolt. According to *Outside* magazine, John saw his first bungee jump on the television show "That's Incredible." John, whose boyhood hero was Evel Knievel, called his brother in 1987 and suggested they jump off the 140-foot bridge at Don Pedro Reservoir near Yosemite. Peter agreed and afterward called it "the most intense thrill I'd ever had in my life." He told *Outside*, "I felt like a spider dropping into the Grand Canyon on a thread."

It was a 140-foot spark. Well, a little less than 140 feet—the idea, after all, was not to hit bottom. But it was a spark, nevertheless, and a year later John quit his job. He thought it would be a good idea to start a bungee-jumping business. He called Peter. "Come on, screw security," he told his brother. "Screw stability and upward mobility. That's not what you're on earth for—to sit there and be calm, to sit there and die slowly."

Peter, the cautious one, was caught. It was the die slowly part. "The saddest thing I ever saw," he told *Outside*, "was the engineers [he worked with] who had stayed 30 years beyond the time they should have gone out and pursued a dream, so I decided to go for it." He opted for personal freedom. Bungee Adventures was born.

The sport of bungee jumping, legend has it, was invented by a woman on Pentecost Island who tricked her abusive husband into suicide. According to local legend, this man chased his wife to a cliff. The woman jumped; so did he. The man fell. The woman, who had tied vines to her legs, had her fall stopped at the last second. From then on, in the village of Bunlap on Pentecost Island, the men decided it would never happen again. All men would learn to jump as proof of manhood and, incidentally, to ensure a good harvest of yams. One spark, and all along it was yams.

But not for the Kockleman brothers, who used the technologically advanced bungee cords rather than vines. Their spark was the need for total commitment of body, soul, and mind. They prove that even the craziest thing, if it's something you love, can be quite logical. Let me explain. Bungee jumping is actually a mechanical exercise that involves many things, including Peter's engineering skills. All these things must be factored into every jump—the height of the jump, the weight of the jumper, the length of the cords. The Kocklemans' image of being the best is really a result of creative logic—primal energy harnessed to create extraordinary events, bungee jumps.

The Kocklemans are the kings of bungee jumping and heroes of the famous Don't-try-this-yourself bungee-jumping sneaker commercial for the Reebok Pump. In three weeks the commercial was banned.

But it was an eye-catching commercial. The idea was to show how the Pump fits snugger than an ordinary sneaker. Both brothers stood on a bridge. One brother pumped his

Pumps. The other brother wore another brand—no pump. They both jumped. At the end the commercial showed the brother with the Pumps hanging upside down from his bungee cord. And then it showed the other cord—empty.

What it showed me, though, was two brothers making money doing what they love. That's what a good spark will get you.

Someone once said, "Search the parks in all the cities and you will never find a statue of committees." Committees do not create sparks; they drown them. Only an individual spawns the vision. And that's what the spark is, really—a vision. Without a vision, nothing happens. Vision is not external but internal—a mirror holds the key.

A climber I know failed on his two greatest climbs—K2 and Mt. Everest—because at the last minute he lost conviction in himself and his vision. This man seemed to have everything all good climbers do—strength, determination, and a cerebral appreciation of nature and man's minute role in it.

As a challenge beyond just climbing, he decided to organize and lead some major climbs. This is quite an involved process. It includes fund-raising, procuring permits, and selecting team members. It also involves leadership—pairing up climbers, deciding the route, and adjusting to the inevitable surprises that occur on a major climb. It is a very tiring role.

In both of his failures the same thing happened. He had done everything perfectly. He was well organized, and everything went well as his group pushed to the last camp before the final assault on the peak. But as is always the case, conditions were harsh. At the last moment, when all the pieces were in place for a fine-tuned effort by a group with a singular goal, he wavered. He didn't lead. Each time there was more than one possible route to take. Rather than deciding, the leader put it up to a vote. Well, some people, on thinking about it, wanted to go one way. Others wanted to go the other way. Some were shooting for personal firsts, others for world recognition. People were tired, tempers were short. The air was nearly impossible to breathe. And the leader said, "How about a vote?"

What happened should be obvious to anyone who has been through a crisis, business or otherwise. The team fell apart. They split up and went their own ways. Some went back down. Those who went forward failed to reach the peak—without teamwork and support they were doomed to failure.

The point is, democracy doesn't work at 8,000 meters, and it doesn't work in a crisis. Sometimes you just have to tell people exactly what to do and they will gladly accept it. The climber who organized these climbs was still in the decision stage when he should have been in the action stage. He let the group of climbers vote on two different approaches and inevitably ended up with dissatisfied climbers who had nothing more to give when their route wasn't chosen. There is a difference between management and leadership, and there are clear points when a leader must lead.

This just further illustrates why there are no statues of committees. This is not to say that democracy is bad. As I will show later, it is essential that leaders tap into the knowledge of others to be successful. However, at some point you have to open up and be honest. Don't kid yourself—leading is not easy. You have to want to be a leader or you will find the sacrifices required are too great. Don't take the role of a leader for its celebrity, because if you only rise to the bait to be liked and adored, you probably will never want to or be capable of making tough decisions. Leaders must make tough decisions, long before there is certainty. A leader scrutinizes all doubts and then, if his conviction doesn't waver, presses on toward the goal. At that point the adventure accelerates.

Morris L. West said in *The Shoes of a Fisherman*, "It takes so much to be a full human being that there are few who have the enlightenment or the courage to pay the price. . . . One has to abandon altogether the search for security and reach out to the risk of living with both arms. One has to accept pain as a condition of existence. One has to court doubt and darkness as the cost of knowing."

Or, as John Kockelman told his brother, "Screw stability."

Take that next step. Bill Gates, the phenomenally successful founder of Microsoft, described his role as president of the company as follows: "My job is to have a vision and communicate it."

How simple. But of course it isn't, or the entire world would be successful. The reason it isn't is not that people lack visions. All people, if they are honest, have some visions. But so often you are told, implicitly or explicitly, that the vision is impossible. "Don't try that," others say. And if you do, they warn you to be sure you have something to fall back on. So often, someone tries to drown your vision in their embalming fluid.

But you have to dig below the day-to-day bottom line of security and analyze your life in a linear format. You know the past. You know the present. The future is up to you. What is it that you really want from life? Honestly?

There is one more question: What are you going to do about it?

Robert Noyes knew. He decided early on in his career

that a nonexistent technology could be invented, and that it would be marketable.

Noyes is generally considered the father of the semiconductor industry. A semiconductor is what replaced the old vacuum tubes that were in radios and televisions. The technology has since evolved into the computer chip and fueled high-tech industry around the world.

Noyes was convinced that semiconductor technology could revolutionize electronics. Beyond that, he was convinced that he was the one to lead the charge. His belief was based on two things: the logic from his academic work at Stanford University and a near-religious belief in himself and his vision. His vision did not so much see the future as create it.

And creating the future is the reason for the spark. What good is a great idea that dies unborn in a risk-free and terribly bored mind? Without the logic to make it work, an idea is useless—an intellectual miscarriage.

Every vision does not have to be a grand one on the scale of a new industry. Small visions are equally valid. What's important is not the size of the vision but the honesty of it and the commitment to it.

One of my favorite small visions came from one person within a large company, Northwestern Mutual Life Insurance. As in most large companies, the employees complained about the constant ringing of their phones. Anybody who works near a phone can relate to this problem. Just when you get going on something—just when you get that inner roll we all strive for—the phone rings.

After analysis, it turned out at Northwestern Mutual Life that most of the bothersome calls were internal. This is a humorous irony—employees trying to get things done were keeping other employees from getting their work done. Certainly most of the calls were important. Still, those doing the calling were also complaining about being called. In essence, efficiency was hurt by employees trying to be more efficient. An unsolvable dilemma, right? Of course not. What Northwestern Mutual Life did was set aside one day a week—Thursday—for no internal phone calls. If you have a question on Thursday, hold it. Move on to something else. Don't bother anyone, and no one will bother you. It worked marvelously. People were happier, and efficiency went way up.

This next story is great because it shows how a little ingenuity coupled with the good fortune of being at the right place at the right time will reap untold rewards for someone with foresight. I have a friend who was a ski instructor, bartender, and construction worker in Vail when that resort first started to grow. One of his jobs was to build the Vail jail—not much more than a few holding cells for those fun-loving people who got a bit too rowdy on a Saturday night.

As he was building the jail, my friend began to contemplate his own Saturday-night tendencies—he, like many of my friends, had an affinity for good times. In other words, he thought as he was laying the bricks, it wouldn't hurt to plan ahead. Sure enough, not long after the jail was built my friend managed to get himself arrested for a little Rocky Mountain rowdiness at a local bar. But as I said, this story is about foresight—vision, if you will. When my friend was building the jail, he had left one brick loose and hidden a key to the cell behind it. By the time the sheriff got back to the bar where he had arrested my friend, he found my friend already there entertaining everybody with his tale of a "daring" jail-house escape.

Another small but effective vision was that of Glen

Plake. Basically, Plake wanted to ski for a living. The problem, obviously, was that lots of people would like to ski for a living. Being a instructor is not very lucrative. He aimed higher. To start with, he went into extreme skiing—that is, skiing out past civilization onto mountains only accessed by hiking, climbing, or helicopters. But a lot of people had already gotten into extreme skiing. In fact, some were even paying money to go extreme skiing. Plake wanted to be paid, rather than pay.

What he did was incredibly simple—he differentiated himself. He went visual. Instead of assuming the clean-cut, all-American look that most skiers go for, Plake became a sort of Sid Vicious on snow. He cut his hair into a spiked mohawk and colored it orange, yellow, and blue. He began to market himself as an image of an extreme skier with character. The ski companies, for example K-2, loved it. They hired him for posters. Filmmakers also found the new image incredibly attractive. He has become a wealthy, and happy, professional skier.

Small visions, when done for the right reasons, work. And better yet, they lead to bigger visions.

It happened to us at The North Face. In 1972 we analyzed the company and realized that most of our sales were in the summer. That made sense. People do the most outdoor activities in the summer. But we wanted to balance our business and cash flow.

We asked ourselves: What do our customers like to do in the winter? One obvious answer was cross-country skiing. It was a natural for those who like to go off into the back country. But from a business perspective it didn't make sense. The number of people who cross-country skied on the West Coast, where we were located, was just too low for a major investment.

We theorized the low number was not because of lack of interest—people love the outdoors summer or winter. The problem was there was nowhere to go—people wanted easy access to a beautiful place with trails. But on the West Coast there were no places with prepared trails or instructors.

Suddenly our small vision of a better wintertime cash flow became a lot bigger. The only way to create a demand for cross-country skis and clothing was to actually create the market in the western United States. The only way to do that was to get trails built.

I was never one to go after anything but the biggest and best, so we aimed for Yosemite National Park. We figured we needed a setting that was so spectacular it would almost sell itself to potential cross-country skiers. The thousand-foot vertical granite walls of Yosemite were a natural enticing backdrop for what we envisioned. All we had to do was convince the park concessionaires to develop a cross-country-skiing program. We were excited.

Then we met them. The concessionaires thought our idea was "intriguing," but they rejected it. It was another committee fiasco. We met again—same thing. No problem, we thought. Just persevere. And we did. Finally they relented. "Great," they said. "Yosemite will be glad to go ahead with the project. Only one thing. We'd like you to do all the work." They wanted us to lay out the trails, get the equipment, find the instructors, and help promote the program. I guess they thought that would deter us. They thought wrong. It energized us.

I worked with Dave Harvey, one of our employees. Dave is an energetic dreamer—the kind of person who makes vision become fact. Dave had gone to school with Johannes von Trapp, youngest son of the von Trapp family, around whom the story *The Sound of Music* had been written. When the von Trapps came to the United States after escaping the Nazis, they opened a chalet in Stowe, Vermont. They offered meals, entertainment by the family, and cross-country skiing—something they had learned in their native Austria. The program was a success, and Johannes became a businessman specializing in cross-country skiing.

Through Dave, we asked Johannes to help us. He was a lifelong cross-country skier. He was about six feet, three inches tall, rail thin, and a sort of philosophic mountain man. He had intelligence, experience, business savvy, and a perfect image for our new endeavor. Also, he knew some unemployed potential instructors. One of them was a young man named Ned Gillette, who had been a member of the 1968 U.S. Olympic ski team. Remember that name—Ned Gillette—it will come up again before I finish this book. Gillette's whole life is a metaphor for what I am trying to say.

Anyway, Johannes had more to offer than just image and names. He knew how to lay out ski trails, and he knew what the American cross-country skier wanted. We listened, we learned, and we started a business. Ultimately, in fact, the winter business for The North Face exceeded that of the summer.

What happens when a spark hits—as it inevitably does with every human—is that there is a choice. Take it seriously or ignore it. At The North Face, we took it seriously. Why not improve winter cash flow? Why can't cross-country skiing become popular? Why not lay out ski trails in Yosemite National Park? As George Bernard Shaw once said, "You see things and say why, but I dream of things that never were and say, why not."

If you take the spark seriously, it then becomes necessary to manifest the vision. One of my favorite songs is "Teach Your Children," by Crosby, Stills, Nash & Young. It begins with these words: "You, who are on the road, must have a code that you can live by . . ." A code to live by—what a beautiful, touching concept. But it is so difficult to keep your code—to remain true to yourself. It becomes so easy to make little compromises—rationalizations, if you will—because of your fear of the consequences. But little compromises very quickly become big compromises if you are not careful. Put differently, if you have something to fall back on (a little compromise), you will fall back on it (a huge compromise).

And so there is, inevitably, a test of the vision. Are you tough enough and true enough to stick with your vision?

I once sailed off the Adriatic coast of Yugoslavia with a ruddy-faced captain who told some incredible stories. His name was Ian.

Ian loved to sail. When he was younger, he told me, he didn't have enough money to own a boat. But still, he dreamed. His were not idle daydreams—he used logic to make his goal a reality. His goal was to be a charter captain. One day while crossing the English Channel, he saw the boat of his dreams—a 62-foot wooden ketch. Ian turned to his wife and instantly told her that someday he would own that exact boat. First he had to find out who owned the boat. It took a while, but he eventually found the owner. Then he had to raise funds and convince the owner to sell that beautiful boat. Neither was an easy task. It took him three years to raise the money and almost as long to convince the owner to sell the boat. "So, how do you like her?" he asked when he finished that story. I was riding on his dream boat.

Ian told me another story that day. On one of his early voyages across the Atlantic—sailing from the Caribbean to

England—he encountered a horrendous storm, with 40- to 50-foot waves. When he was down below, he felt the boat slide down one of those huge waves. Suddenly he heard a loud bang—it sounded to him as if the bottom had been torn from the boat. He was shaken. He had an urgent pull in his stomach, and he raced to lift up the floorboards for a look. It was frightening—what would he find?

What he found, incredibly, was that everything was fine. The noise he had heard was simply the engine jump starting—it was caused by the propeller being spun as the boat rode down the wave.

Relieved, he went up on deck to tell his wife what had happened. She had been at the wheel. But when Ian went on deck, his wife was nowhere to be found. He went into a panic—at least at first. This was the one person who shared his dream. She did not just share the dream; she was an integral part of it. Without her, there was no dream. She was everything. And she apparently had been thrown from the boat.

It was pouring. The night was pitch black. The wind was howling, the waves were monstrous. Ian called out her name. He screamed it. But the night was so loud and ominous it was to no avail. He had that same urgent pull in his stomach—only tenfold. She was lost somewhere in the Atlantic.

Quickly logic came to the fore. Ian executed a perfect figure-eight rescue move that sailors are taught. Then he proceeded directly back on the line he believed they had taken. Thirty minutes later, miraculously, he spotted her and pulled her aboard. She was safe! Admittedly, she had some broken ribs and a minor case of hypothermia. But their dream was safe.

It was ten years later when he told me that story—

laughing the whole way through it. "The point is," he said, "she still sails with me." His was a religious belief in his dream—one that said risking everything is worth the chance to get everything. And it was backed up by a purely logical approach to his craft—sailing. He found out how tough it could be, and he passed the test.

It all comes from the spark. I had a plumber come by to fix a water leak in my house. What he did really didn't interest me, but it sure interested him. His vision may have appeared small to me. But tracking his way through a maze of pipes was to him a fantastic way to make money. His wasn't a giant spark across the sky like the Kocklemans', but it was just as legitimate a spark. His took the form of a short conquest—a water heater and a set of pipes. When I looked at the plumbing, I hadn't a clue. He was the man of the moment.

These are not just stories about people who were determined to be successful, and so they were. There is a point. The reason people are successful is because they work to get the spark. They are not afraid to follow it, and they are not afraid of asking others to follow. It does not just magically occur in some and lie dormant in others. It is, once again, a combination of logic and inspiration—conveyed to others with infectious optimism. Either one without the other is bound to fall short of a true goal. Logic and hard work without inspiration will lead only to a tedious existence. On the other hand, there is nothing more wasteful than a lazy dreamer.

Tom and Priscilla Wrubel could easily have been lazy dreamers, and no one would have even noticed. No one, that is, except themselves. Tom was an architect who owned a plant store. He had a degree in architecture, but he wasn't satisfied with it. The plant store was sort of a steppingstone for him and Priscilla—not really what they wanted, but closer to it than architecture. They wanted to make money showing his appreciation of nature. And they wanted to educate others to appreciate it also.

The problem with the plant store was it didn't really help preserve nature, and it wasn't unique. It was basically a cookie-cutter occupation. So they kept thinking. What was it? What could it be that they were looking for? Slowly the idea began to take shape: a store that sold gifts that celebrated nature, optics for stargazing and bird watching, blow-up dinosaurs, gift cards with natural settings and materials, and fossil reproductions. They wanted to create awareness. They wanted a nice place to work that they could be proud to call their own. They didn't want to evangelize about preserving nature; they wanted people to enjoy themselves as they became aware. Their overall goal was commitment.

The Nature Company is now a chain of retail stores doing in excess of $100 million a year in sales. The stores are great—a celebration of nature, and of the Wrubels' vision. Water trickles and falls throughout the stores. The walls are a light wood. Nature tapes of wind, and rain, and animals play through speakers. It is a deep-forest ambience. There is even dappled light, just as you would experience walking among tall trees on a sunny day.

It would have been easy for Tom to use his architecture degree and maintain a nice, secure life. Or he and Priscilla could have pretended to be satisfied by his plant shop. But they found their spark and lived by it.

It is a wonderful thing to see the physical truth of a dream that once existed only in someone's mind. It is a powerful, fluid event as the thought process works, as something great evolves and becomes reality.

I was once told the story of a window dresser for Macy's in New York City. The man was very good at his craft. He had earned a reputation for doing the most visible, the most daring, the most eye-catching displays in the entire city. But Macy's continued to challenge him. It was leadership at its best—a great talent challenged to go the extra step, from interesting to brilliant.

This man was to do a display of Macy's new kitchen set—a table, chairs, china, stemware, everything. So he did. He set a beautiful table; the whole nine yards. I believe it even had a realistic-looking turkey on a tray. His boss came to look at it. "That's great," he said. "I like it. Really interesting. But you know, I'd like something more. Something different. It has the promise of greatness. Why don't you do it again?"

The window dresser was dumbfounded. It seemed great, he thought. What more could he do? But he kept thinking. What more indeed? He went outside and looked in at the window, analyzing the perspective of the shopper. Thinking it out, staring. Mentally he began putting different pieces in different places. Suddenly, exactly like a spark, it hit him. What if, he thought, the entire display were glued and wired together so it could be turned on its side—suspended in air? What if the shopper walking down the street could look in the window at the wall and actually be looking down on the entire display, as if from an overhead camera?

And so it was. The table and chairs were hung on their sides. The china, napkins, etc., were glued to the table. And the display was incredible.

That's how it is where logic meets religion—hard work becomes the stuff of genius. You don't have to be a genius to be a genius. You just have to want it badly enough, and you can't be deterred by criticism. You have to be an 800-pound gorilla in a 100-pound world.

One such person was Howard Head. An aircraft engineer during World War II, Head became fascinated with skiing in 1947. It was a fun sport, but Head wanted more. He was frustrated by the immobility of the heavy wooden skis, and he was certain he could make better skis.

Aluminum! That was the answer. The spark came in an instant. The skis took a while to design. Quite a while. He had a number of problems with the prototypes. But he kept thinking about aluminum skis—skiing on aluminum skis—having all his colleagues at such places as Tuckerman's Ravine test his prototype aluminum skis. The spark was ever constant.

When he finally perfected aluminum skis, Head Ski flourished. Another one of those "overnight" successes—it took years. At one point Head captured more than 70 percent of the market. But sparks sometimes fade or are replaced by other sparks, and in Head's case it was the latter—the even newer spark of fiberglass skis.

Head Ski faltered, and the investors panicked. Head was edged out and replaced by a committee, a professional management team conspicuously devoid of industry knowledge. A familiar story. The management team purged the company of the knowledgeable people Howard Head had assembled to carry out his vision. Head Ski, under its new management, lost more market share. Five years later none of the new management team was around. They were off helping other companies with the experience they had gained at the expense of Head. Head was sold to AMF.

What of Howard Head, who had been branded nothing more than an entrepreneur despite meteoric success? At the age of 60 he took up tennis and never looked back. A new spark hit him, and a new adventure commenced. He became determined to build a better tennis racket and took over Prince. He was frustrated by the shots he "just missed," so he designed the world's first oversize tennis racket. Once again he revolutionized an industry. He became a leader again and proved his leadership skills, which finally culminated in a highly profitable sale of the company to Cheeseborough-Ponds.

Sparks are not just for the young, but they are born of the energy of youth. They are the fluid essence of adventure, and if you follow them in their truest state, they will lead you not just to success, but to understanding.

4

Testing the Spark:

Eye to Eye with Those You Love

Helen Thayer imagined the crunch. It would sound like a chomp on a frozen chocolate bar with nuts, maybe. Or perhaps there would be more of a hollow crackle, like large crickets squished underfoot—in an empty gymnasium. *Cccc-rrrrr-uuuuuuunch!*

The bear had lain in wait behind a 30-foot mound of ice in the Arctic Circle. Thayer was on a sled behind a dog named Charlie. Suddenly the bear lurched from behind the mound. It was huge—bigger than a skyscraper, with wide, furry limbs and massive, angry teeth. It roared. Thayer backed away slowly. It slapped her sled. She was in awe. It just tossed the sled over with a wave of its paw.

"In that moment [when she first saw the bear] I realized that all I knew meant nothing," she told *Ms.* magazine. "I learned that in the face of that magnificent, killing creature, my gun might as well have been a toothpick and that I was no more important than the tiniest speck of snow. I knew if he got my head in his mouth, there'd be a very loud crunch."

She was on the last legs of her journey when she ran into the bear. She was returning from becoming the first woman to ever go solo to the magnetic North Pole. This bear was not the first she had run into on the trip. But it was the meanest.

She had no choice but to unleash Charlie. Charlie was a gift, a bullish, black husky-Newfoundland mix given to her just before she took off on the trip. He was a brave, loyal friend—a cunning, tundra-wise scout raised on Cornwallis Island in Canada's Northwest Territories by an Inuit polar bear hunter. A dog raised by a polar bear hunter; Charlie turned out to be a most wonderful gift.

It was when Thayer was thinking about the crunch that Charlie made his move. Charlie used his speed to get at the legs of the bear. Charlie bit and danced. The bear became confused. Charlie held on. The bear spun around, reaching to slap Charlie as it had the sled. But Charlie was quicker, holding on and spinning faster. Around and around they went. Thayer stared as it all moved in front of her in the slow motion of urgency. Each heartbeat seemed to take hours, yet it went so fast.

Finally the bear freed himself, and Charlie took off running. The bear, who moments earlier had been staring at Thayer as if she were dinner at the Ritz, took off after Charlie.

She blinked.

They were gone. Charlie and the bear. Barking and growling and racing over the tundra, just like two wild animals in the wilderness.

The barking and growling disappeared. Thayer waited. A minute, two. Five minutes, ten—nothing. She stood, breathing. Thinking. She was forcing her will on events out of sight, beyond control. *Charlie will be back. Charlie will be back*, she told herself.

A half hour later Charlie finally reappeared. He was panting. His coat was sweaty, even in the Arctic cold. But he was happy—his tail wagged. Thayer knew the bear was gone, and the two of them, woman and dog, breathed in the air like champagne.

They had transcended the barrier that divides humans from animals. They had connected. Each had bought into the vision of a joint quest to the magnetic North Pole. Officially the 27-day journey over 345 miles of bleak landscape was the first-ever solo effort by a woman. But Thayer knows better. Solo? Hell no; she did it with Charlie.

Friendship is not something to be taken lightly in the world of adventuring. Likewise, connections should not be taken lightly in the world of business, or in any world. The friendship of a human and a dog can accomplish great things. Imagine the potential of a human-to-human connection.

When I was 18, I had a 3.9 grade-point average and an opportunity to play football on scholarship for the local Spokane community college. I had also been accepted at Stanford—no scholarship. At the community college I would be a star quarterback. I knew that. At Stanford, I could try out for the team. I was five foot eight. I was fast, and I had a pretty good arm. But I was five foot eight.

What to do? Well, accepting a scholarship was out of the

question in my proud and well-to-do family. But still, I could be a star. From day one I wanted to be a pro athlete. I wanted to be really good at something. I didn't like mediocrity. And the easiest, clearest picture of excelling is in athletics.

One night, when I was out having some beers with a friend of mine in the mountains around Spokane, she looked right at me and told me the nicest thing anyone had ever said up to that point. "You stupid shit," she said. "You have an opportunity to go to Stanford, one of the best schools in the country, and you're thinking of throwing it away so you can be a star for two more years." She was one of my best friends. Not a girlfriend. A friend.

"You're out of your mind," she said. "You're never going to play football professionally, and to pass up that opportunity is crazy."

Generally I listen to my friends when I feel a true connection. Advice without a friendship is not a connection. It has an ulterior motive.

When my friends talk, it may take a while to reach me, because always I trust my instinct first. But I've tried my best to avoid a personal Vietnam where I made a decision and followed it so blindly that I trusted no one. When somebody you love is telling you something from his or her own heart and not trying to sell you a bill of goods, you hear it. You may not agree, but it definitely comes into play.

When I sold The North Face, the advice of friends was quite helpful. Selling was a tremendously difficult decision. I had spent 20 years building it, and I felt there were hundreds of things left to accomplish. It was like one of my children. But finances were thin, and I needed to raise quite a bit of money to finance the growth I planned. In addition, one of my ex-employees, whom I had fired, was a shareholder. This man had a personal vendetta against me. He fabricated things about me and the company when talking to other shareholders. He wanted to get the company sold—probably more for his ego than economics. He even suggested to some that once I was gone, he would be a perfect replacement. On that point no one took him seriously—his subpar record from working in the company was well known.

But it was tumultuous. A dissident minority spearheaded by this self-serving ex-employee wanted out of the company. It was them or me. Either I bought them out and financed the growth, or they would sell their shares to someone undesirable. We held board meetings constantly—full of intrigue and uncertainty. But I had a narrow majority on my side, and I arranged financing for the buy out and for our planned growth from a variety of sources (banks, foreign partners, personal funds, etc.). Finally I was in a position to execute the buy out. But the whole situation bothered me. I was borrowing all the money. I had to guarantee everything. If, somehow, things didn't work out, I would be personally bankrupt and a lot of my friends would lose their jobs.

The risk didn't bother me—at least no more than usual. Risk, after all, is risk. Interest rates could go up, the economy could go bad. The risk was there. The challenge didn't bother me—I was ready to take it on, and I was ready to take on the ex-employee with the personal vendetta. But something was wrong. I knew it, but I wouldn't admit it. I couldn't put it into words. Something, just something.

At this point I talked to four of my directors, all personal friends. Each approached me at different times. They said it differently, but each had a common theme: "You don't look like you're having fun anymore," they said. "Why bother with the additional debt and with restructuring the company? Why not get out and move on to something you can enjoy?"

There it was. I had always told myself I would get out when it was no longer fun. My friends were right. The connection clarified everything. The fun was gone. Too many negatives had gone into the buy out, too many new worries had been added. I thought long and hard. In many ways it hurt to sell the company. But I took a deep breath, and I did it. I never looked back. I went skiing with my family.

Listening, rather than blindly going about your own course, is extremely important. If you are an evolving individual, you must be adaptable. You have to have an ego check to understand whether a goal is more ego driven than reality driven. Ego, after all, can be blinding. From perspective comes knowledge, and no one has a corner on knowledge.

It is important to know the perspective of the person offering advice. For instance, someone who went through the Depression has a completely different mind-set from those generations born since the 1930s. But just as important as their life perspective is their perspective to you. The people to trust are those you love and those who love you. Some would say it is best to trust only those who have nothing to gain by giving you advice—the people who think more about you than their image or their job. But often it is also important to test your ideas with those they affect most—those whose lives are riding on your decisions. In business it is important to test ideas with friends completely outside the company as well as employees and family. If you can make a connection with those giving the advice, the input is invaluable.

Ralph Keeney is one of the world's foremost authorities on decision analysis, yet when faced with a major decision affecting his own life, he found it very important to test the spark—to assign values to the wants, needs, and aspirations in his life. Keeney has taught at Harvard, Stanford, and the Massachusetts Institute of Technology and has worked all over the world. He also does regular consulting for government and business on critical decision making. His is a rational, reasoned approach.

And so it was when he was offered an attractive, tenured professorship at the University of Southern California in Los Angeles. At first glance it had everything, both economic and professional rewards. But there was another part of his life equally important—his personal life. His wife, Janet Beach, is a very successful marketing executive, having been in charge of marketing at such companies as Levi Strauss and U.S. Sprint.

When Keeney was offered the job at USC, his wife had recently formed her own company in San Francisco, called U.S. Marketing Services. They also had a young son and a spectacular apartment in San Francisco overlooking all the bridges.

What to do? Keeney treated the issue like all the other decisions he analyzes. He put together a matrix of all the factors affecting the decision from his perspective and weighted them according to his values. Then he tested the spark. He went to Janet—who certainly had a vested interest in his decision. He asked her to also give her input. He logically expressed it and systematically plugged it into his matrix. She wanted to stay in San Francisco. He wanted the job. A dilemma, right?

Not really. They talked. They weighed their lives, their individual goals, and their shared goals. They thought about options and came up with a workable answer—he would accept the job, but only if he could do his work from San

Francisco. They wouldn't move, and he wouldn't commute. He had a young son he wanted to spend time with, and he didn't want to tear Janet away from her business—and he liked San Francisco too. He thought about such an arrangement from USC's perspective and created ways to contribute his share to meeting the university's goals. They presented their conclusion to USC. Different as it was, the school accepted it.

It was their friendship that made such a solution possible. If either one had been blind to the other's goals, it could have caused difficulties. But they analyzed the problem. They looked at it from the perspective of each. And they were honest. They recognized that they have both dual goals and separate goals. Each was supportive on both counts.

Once I was skiing at Vail with a lot of notables from the ski industry. Somehow I ended up in a group of former racers, downhill-speed-skiing record holders and Olympic hopefuls. They took off down the hill, leaving me in a swirl of powder. I was apprehensive, but I took off after them. As I was picking my way down the hill I noticed they had stopped about halfway down to wait for me.

Until then I had been skiing at a relaxed pace, picking my line down the hill, and looking for soft snow to turn on, skiing conservatively. But seeing them waiting for me fired my competitive juices. I hated being left behind. I wanted to prove something. Boy, did I. I had this vision—I was going to show them. Instead of carefully skiing down to where they were, I would give it my all, let it go as it were, and fly past them as they stood impressed by my skills. Oh, to dream.

But life is often a bit different. I took off, all right. Zoom! I was flying. But just as I approached them, I started to rethink it. The seven metal pins in my left leg from a prior skiing accident flashed into my mind. I was an adequate skier; they were the best. Not a good idea, I thought. Slow down. I edged my skis into the hill, turning right. I did it at the wrong time. My downhill ski caught on a hard mogul and I was thrown in the air. I did a flip and, incredibly, landed upright on my skis. I came to a stop right in front of the group. I looked at them, acting as if I had planned the entire thing. I thought I had them fooled. Yeah, I thought, I can fit in with these people.

One of my friends skied up to me. He put his hand on my shoulder and pulled me away from the group. "You're in way over your head," he said, stating the obvious. "Why don't you just free-ski down the hill by yourself? It will probably be best for all of us."

I could've continued the but-I-planned-the-flip act. But I didn't. He was being honest. He was my friend. And he was right. Friends do not falsely encourage you any more than they falsely discourage you. Friends connect with you and tell you the truth. They help you winnow fact from fiction.

Friends tell you when you are going wrong. When you go right, a friend is there and supports you. Friendship is the nature of life. An absolute connection like that of Helen Thayer and her dog, Charlie, can create magical moments of self-realization. A friendship is something to test the spark. If a friend truly has your interests at heart, nine times out of ten the friend, like Charlie, will affirm the vision.

It takes a tremendous understanding of reality to know when a friend with a concern about your vision may be right. The friend may or may not share your vision, but the true friend always understands even if he or she disagrees. True friends tell the truth.

The faith, trust, and eye-to-eye honesty of friendship is an absolute necessity for success. Concrete goals are fine, but they must be balanced by abstract rewards. As life moves on, you have to savor those rewards—they are the nutrients of the soul. They inspire you to tackle the seemingly quixotic challenges of leadership.

These rewards are like the feeling you get when you see a baby for the first time, or when you kiss your lover or sink a 20-foot putt. Such a reward is an intoxication of spirit—a joyful tattoo on the soul.

Those connections are a power source, like an electrical outlet that works both ways—both giving and receiving energy. It is that way for Helen Thayer and Charlie.

It is also that way, only more so, for Thayer and her husband, Bill. They are both adventurers. Theirs is not a one-way street. It is not as if one acts out dreams and the other supports those. They both go on adventures—sometimes together, and sometimes alone. They both dream, they both support, they both give and take energy. It is like perpetual motion, this love of theirs, giving more energy than it takes away—and it takes away plenty. Adventuring, after all, is not for the meek.

Another connection pursued by Thayer is one many adventurers pursue. Far too few companies, however, recognize this type of pursuit as an enormous opportunity. It is an immeasurable loss for those that don't pursue these connections.

For her next expedition Thayer is planning to give something back in the form of a huge connection. Adventurers often do give something back, with articles and speeches. But her next adventure, to ski to the magnetic North Pole, will be much more. With a satellite linkup the Thayers (both will go on this adventure) will transmit progress of their trip daily to 100 schools in 40 countries. They will collect samples for scientific research, and students will be able to see the data. On their return all expedition equipment, in addition to slides and videos, will go into classrooms nationwide. The couple will also lecture at schools across the country.

The Thayers have recognized a basic truism of life: Giving is better than receiving. Sure, it's a cliché. But it is applicable and proven. A huge connection is what makes a mind-set, a symphony—a religion. It works, especially in business. It brings prosperity—for the wallet *and* the soul.

The cold-fish, impersonal training of MBAs and lawyers doesn't work anymore. Long revered in business circles, the detached executive and antiseptic style of management is obsolete. Maybe it worked for short-term money. Maybe it worked in a fascist system that never recognized the toll of wasted potential and shattered lives. Over the long run it never really worked, not in a way that could ally itself with basic humanity.

A company must recognize that success is not about products; it's about people. People determine a company's success. People, after all, make the products. To care for people is to care about what they do—to understand their psyche, to move beyond business into the realm of humanity.

Recognizing the soul of a company is one thing. Acting on this and making sure it is inculcated into every individual is another. Vision equals cause.

At The North Face in 1987 we had a problem—disposal of discounted product and seconds. The traditional method of dealing with such excess was to discount it, offer it to dealers, and hope. Hope someone would take it off our hands and that it would not too adversely impact on our profit margins.

My vice president of retail, Tom Applegate, came to me with a better idea: Hold a retail sale of the excess and give all the profits to the AIDS cause. It was a fabulous idea, one a detached executive could never back. Give profits away? How radical. Giving to AIDS in 1987 was even more radical. Homophobes even within our company fought against the sale. Plus some employees are always awful fearful of unorthodox thinking. Many companies use disagreements as an excuse to do nothing. We certainly had disagreement, but I had to decide if the company would take a stand.

We had four goals. We wanted to raise public AIDS awareness by advertisements, teach people that the illness could strike virtually anyone, increase awareness within our company, and also move merchandise to clear out our warehouse. The cynical would look at that last goal as our only goal. The cynical would be wrong.

At the time AIDS was shunned by most of society as strictly a homosexual disease, which it is not. Applegate reasoned, and he was right, that if the rugged image of The North Face got behind the cause of AIDS awareness, we could accomplish all four goals.

We sold almost $1 million worth of goods at a profit, which we donated. But even more important, from a business standpoint, was that we gained the loyalty and respect of a lot of customers. It was another way of getting people to identify with The North Face. It was our way of identifying with ourself. I had people at the cash registers ask if I could find more things for them to buy. They wanted to help out. What meant the most to me, though, was the reaction of my employees. For numerous reasons—the adventures we sponsored, the quality we created, the camaraderie of the group—our employees always identified with our company. After the benefit I heard my favorite words in the world:

"You know, Hap," I was told by numerous employees, "I'm proud to work for The North Face."

Depending on a company's orientation and type of business, less controversial issues could be used as a rallying point. In 1987 the AIDS issue was controversial. However, I felt good about taking such a stand. Not only was it right; it gave our company an image that made us all proud.

Controversy is not bad. It can be great if you are right. The world is full of controversy. Remember, lots of people are on the "wrong" side of issues. If you don't stand for something, you stand for nothing.

It is possible to avoid controversial issues and still get involved. McDonald's, for instance, has done a wonderful job with the Special Olympics as well as with their support of the Ronald McDonald foundation for children with critical illnesses. General Mills and the Rockefeller family have put together great art collections that are shown around the country. Mobil and Exxon have for years sponsored public television because executives at those companies realize that caring builds business.

People don't want faceless companies. They want something to identify with, and when they find a company that they relate to, they will gladly wear a T-shirt splashing the company's name across the front and back—advertising at no cost the good deeds of that company. If people care about what you care about and vice versa, you have made at the very least a visceral connection.

The public is becoming aware of issues, voting with their pocketbooks. Just look at the environmentalist movement, which is gaining strength around the world. Anita Roddick, managing director of the 620-store Body Shops, understands this. She also understands that a company can make a difference in the world, and she is among a growing list of entrepreneurs who are using their financial prowess to change things for the betterment of society.

Although she sells cosmetics, she appeals less to her customers' vanity than to their concern for the environment and social issues. Hers is a green machine, a capitalistic engine rolling forth for causes such as Amnesty International, the rain forest, and recycling.

Capitalism and liberal causes can coexist, just as a business life and a nonbusiness life can. In fact, if one is to be successful, it is imperative to have one life, not two.

Unfortunately many businesspeople have divided their business life from the rest of their life. Many think of themselves as compassionate and caring individuals, even when the companies they lead are not. It is an attempt at a moral separation. It never works.

And many have also separated their private life from their business life. Nothing is worse—it sends a message that at work it is okay not to care. Those who attempt to justify the dichotomy—say they split their shoddy business practices from their private lives so as not to poison their home environment. But the concept of separation in reality creates a quagmire with no escape. It just gets deeper.

A lot of wealthy fat cats seem quite content despite their shoddy business dealings. But you cannot somehow count only part of your life on your moral scorecard. It all counts—the good, the bad, and the ugly. If your company is polluting the world yet you recycle at home, are you really making a difference? Yes, unfortunately you sure are.

A private and business life also must be one because each must make sacrifices to the other. They can be nurturing partners or cannibalistic.

From a business standpoint you must integrate your private and business life so you can viscerally know your people and they know you. If you want to lead them to greatness, you must be more than a cardboard cutout to them. Only in that way can you make that magical connection and deal with them on a basis of personal understanding.

Lute Jerstad was the second American to climb Mt. Everest. The story of how he made the final assault is a testament to trust.

As he sat in the final camp before the summit, he was tired, and he lacked oxygen. That night he tried to sleep, but it was nearly impossible. The wind whistled by his tent. He was cold, his bones ached like bad weather, and he was anxious to get to the peak. After all, this was Everest!

But the air was thin, and his movements and thinking were sluggish. He gave up on sleep and decided to melt snow over his gas stove for water to stave off dehydration. He turned on the jet of his gas stove, but then his mind wandered. Eventually he looked back at the stove and thought to light it.

Jerstad was lucky. He lived through the explosion of fumes that had filled his tent. But it was a horrible explosion and he was temporarily blinded.

Most people would have given up the climb and just felt lucky to be alive. Most would have sought medical help below. Not Jerstad. This was Everest. He had to make the top.

He pleaded with his Sherpa guide and explained he was blind but strong. "I can make it if you can help," he said. He let out his soul—"this means so much," he said. The guide agreed, and Jerstad put his trust completely in the Sherpa. Jerstad made it to the top of Everest alongside him. When they were at the peak, the Sherpa pulled out a movie camera and he and Jerstad filmed the view, filmed each other, and filmed the accomplishment.

Later, after descending the mountain, Jerstad's vision returned. He watched the film, reveling once again in the conquest.

Trust. It's an easy word to say, a tough thing to gain. It takes honesty. Jerstad knew the guide was no mere employee helping him toward a personal goal. The guide was his ticket to a dream, and in essence the difference between life and death.

Great things are never the result of legal contracts. Human connections make for great things.

Debbie and Mark Ferrari do great things. In the summer she's a cocktail waitress. He works in a salami factory. Their connection is to each other and to the undersea world of South Pacific humpback whales. The Ferraris, with no formal scientific training, while swimming among the gigantic whales, have gathered startling information on mother and calf behavior, group behavior, male aggression, and sex identification. By following the gentle humpbacks year after year, they have stunned the world of marine science.

They connected with each other to work toward the goal of studying the animals, and they connected with the whales themselves to make their research more insightful than mere numbers and graphs. Just like Thayer and Charlie, the Ferraris prove a connection can be across species.

But the greatest connection one can have is with family. Family is not necessarily blood relations; it is soul connections. The people you share your life with are family. In business your family must understand and support your passion for greatness. They must be excited. Otherwise they are a drag to it, and it to them.

Just as you must let your employees feel part of your family, you must let your family feel part of your business. Balance is the key to life.

I'm lucky. I'm in the adventuring business, and that is an easy, fun, and exciting thing to share with my family. Rather than tell someone you love about what you do, it is better to let them experience a part of it. It goes beyond the intellectual into the physical and emotional. Even if it doesn't generate the same feeling for them, it's important for them to understand it.

My family has skied together, flown in hot-air balloons, gone white-water rafting through the Grand Canyon, and explored ancient ruins in the jungles and backcountry of Peru and Guatemala.

My family also worked often at The North Face, helping out, attending functions, and acting as a sounding board. But that was the commercial side. There was another side I wanted them to experience—the spirit of adventuring.

When my children, Kelly and Matt, were in grade school (they are now both adults), we took them to the Mayan ruins in Tikal, deep in the jungles of Guatemala. There was my wife, Margot, my children, myself, and our best friends, the Deweys.

We flew in a battered old DC-3. It was an hour flight of green monotony—a Central American jungle canopy that went on like a great ocean. Suddenly out of nowhere, we saw the Tikal pyramids—200 feet high, cast of stone. Two of them. We began shouting. The flight was rough and noisy, but we were more so. And then it got even better. The pilot, a Guatemalan with two-day's growth of beard, turned the plane almost sideways and we flew between the two peaks. It was incredible, as if we had just discovered Tikal ourselves.

When we landed, one of the plane's tires blew out. The pilot smiled and said something like, "Still got three more."

Dust swirled until the propellers stopped. We looked outside—bright and oppressive, as if under a magnifying glass.

We went out, merged together into a family trying new things with the warmth of an old movie. My family's hotel room was small, 8 by 8 feet, and the four of us became very close. The four Deweys had rented the other room in the hotel. In essence, together we had rented the whole hotel. The entire experience had a rhythm, an easy cadence of warm familiarity. Deep below that it had a shout for joy—a great foundation for family.

We explored, basking in the moment. For three days we climbed ruins, went into temples, read hieroglyphics, and solved the mysteries of life. The conversation was mystic, speculation on the past and the future.

We saw monkeys, birds, and trees. We saw each other. We connected. In the plane on the flight out my daughter, Kelly, turned to me. "That's incredible, what you do for a living," she said. "That's fun."

5

Jumping Off the Fence:

Any Decision Is Better Than No Decision

There we were on the Zambezi River between Zimbabwe and Zambia. It was a beautiful day. The sun was up, and we were in the midst of some of the most spectacular scenery in the world.

We were at work. Every year, rather than hire an agency to shoot the photographs for our catalog, we would bring some employees to an outpost of the world and shoot it ourselves. It was a great chance to save money, test our products, and have fun.

There were eight of us that day who were going to run

the Zambezi, a river that had only been run for the first time six months before. My group of four went ahead. We plotted our strategy.

First, we decided on a marker rock—something to give us a sense of direction. We then decided on a direction. The middle of the river looked fairly safe, but there were some large boulders on either side that could cause serious havoc. Off we went, laughing and whooping giddily—gliding and flying over waves. Our boat folded, twisted, and dropped as we crashed forward. This was serious. Each of us became silent, a mantra of frightened concentration.

Warm spray slapped our faces—a real blow but nevertheless a welcome bath in the equatorial heat. And every few seconds we checked for the marker rock. No problem; we were on course.

When we finished that section of the run, falling back in laughter and satisfaction, we waited for the next group. They just shot out. No direction.

Off they went toward the huge boulders along the side. "Stroke!" I yelled from shore. But no. They were frozen. They were headed straight at disaster. They seemed paralyzed. They had failed to make a decision, and so the river took over. It took the raft and slammed it against a huge rock. The raft was almost vertical, and we held our breath. For an instant we couldn't move, and neither could they.

And then it flipped. A most amazing sight. The raft just flew up in the air, and people were thrown off it like play-school figures. We instantly mobilized.

"Rescue!" we all started yelling. "Rescue!" We shoved off and started to row toward the center of the river.

For a moment the only thing visible was the bottom of the raft. Heads popped up, but then we couldn't see them.

We cut across the river, fighting the current. The current brought the other boat to us. Frantically we tried to count the swimmers. "There's one! There's another! I got him, I got him! Hold on!"

And then, "There are two missing!" Screaming, cursing, praying. "Even if the river sucked them down, they should be up by now!" someone yelled.

Finally it hit us. The raft. "Look under the raft!"

We dove in. And, thankfully, there they were. Safe, in a little cover of oxygen, under the raft.

When we finally reached shore, we realized what had just happened—life at its purest. We sat back, popped open some cold beers, and lit up a big old joint of Mountain Thunder, which is what they call the marijuana down there—for good reason, I might add—and just savored existence. For all of its terror, that experience made the trip worth it. There is something about flirting with death that I have always loved. You feel the nerves on the outside of your body. You tingle.

In an odd way, I suppose, that is why we do these things. In retrospect I would rather my friends had chosen the same line we did—in fact, any line was better than letting the river dictate to them as it did. The Zambezi, after all, is exciting enough without mistakes. But sometimes you just have to make mistakes. You have to make a decision and then react from there. You have to jump.

Even if you don't make a decision, you've made a decision. Just because you stand still doesn't mean the world does—time, like the river above, marches on at its ever-steady pace. And as specific events unfold, time sometimes seems to pick up speed. This acceleration of time is relative to the amount of stress associated with any particular upcoming event. If a deadline is approaching and your mind is stuck in the vapor lock of indecision, time seems to move even faster. If a crisis occurs, there is no time to analyze. It is time for action, particularly if you are the leader. To those stuck on the fence the paralysis is painful in its clarity.

Rick LeMoine could have been stuck on the fence. The truth was, he was stuck in a hurricane. Rick is the owner of Kenyon's Market, a convenience store on Cape Cod. In August 1991, at the height of the tourist season—and with the national senior Babe Ruth World Series taking place in Rick's hometown, Falmouth (thus even more tourists than usual)—Hurricane Bob took a nasty turn north from the Caribbean on a dead-eye path for Cape Cod.

Traditionally most hurricanes, as Cape Codders know, begin off the coast of Africa and then sputter harmlessly around the Atlantic Ocean. Occasionally they slam into the islands of the Caribbean. At worst they hit the southeastern United States—no farther north than the Carolinas. Bob knew nothing of tradition.

And so on Saturday, two days before the hurricane hit, Rick first heard of its existence and the probability that it was coming north. So did every other store owner.

On Sunday, Rick did what everyone did. He taped up his windows to protect the glass from shattering in the expected high winds. News of the hurricane also caused panic buying from the customers.

On Monday morning, when it was apparent that the hurricane was on a direct course for the Cape, Rick knew it was time to mobilize. This was a crisis. He talked to his partner, who owned another store nearby, about buying a generator. The cost was $1,200. His partner told him he was crazy to spend that kind of money when there was no guarantee the power would even go off. But Rick had a hunch.

He made a decision and bought the generator, and he bought and filled nine gas cans. Then he gave an electrician friend a case of beer, and the friend wired the generator into Rick's lights. It was a small generator—it couldn't handle his beer, ice cream, or milk coolers, but it could light three aisles in his store. Those lights would allow him to remain open.

The hurricane hit as scheduled, packing winds of up to 110 miles per hour. Trees were downed everywhere. Water swelled. One sailboat even slammed into the front porch of someone's waterfront house. And, of course, the power went out.

Rick's biggest concern was the perishable items in the store—ice cream, frozen meat, and so on. At noon on Monday, at the height of the hurricane, he took all the ice cream from his store to one of the local schools, which was being used as a shelter. While other stores were watching their ice cream melt, Rick was making points with the community.

Unlike most other stores, Rick's store closed for only two hours—just so that Rick could check on the status of his own home. When the hurricane passed at about 5 p.m., Rick called a local ice company. He knew that power was out, meaning refrigerators weren't working. Thus, ice. He made a decision, asking the ice company to bring all the ice they had to his store. He was told the ice company had plenty of ice, but not enough gas for their trucks to make it to his store and back. Rick made another decision. He was friends with the owner of a local construction firm that had a generator to run their gas pumps. He arranged to fuel up the ice trucks at the construction firm.

The ice truck stayed in his parking lot, running its internal freezer. At one point Monday evening 150 people were in the Kenyon's parking lot waiting to buy ice. That night he sold 3,800 bags of ice. On a busy day in the summer he averages 300 bags.

He did another thing too. Unlike the owners of many stores that somehow managed to get ice, he left his price the same. There were so many people without power that in some locations, Rick heard, people were paying 50 cents just for a small scoop of ice. Even the ice company told him to raise his price. But he figured he was still making a profit; there was no reason to gouge. He knew he was in the grocery business, and the community, for the long haul.

When it was over, despite closing for two hours, the store had had its most profitable day. At the same time it had made a mark as one that doesn't gouge and is responsible to the community.

Tuesday was even better. With all of his frozen hot dogs, hamburger, and sausages thawing quickly, Rick made another decision. He brought the gas grill from home and put it right outside his store. Initially it was to feed his employees. But as soon as he fired it up, a line of customers formed. It didn't end until all of his frozen meats were sold.

The milk company on Cape Code traditionally makes its biggest run of the week on Tuesday. But the Tuesday after the hurricane the milk truck couldn't sell any milk because the power was out to run any store coolers. The truck arrived at Kenyon's Market hours earlier than normal. Kenyon's was the last stop of the day, and the driver told Rick no one had bought anything from him. He expected Rick to say the same. But Rick had a better idea.

"Let me have your whole truck," Rick said.

The driver didn't understand. Rick explained. "Let me keep your truck on my lot and we can sell milk right out of it. After all, you have nowhere to go and your truck is refrigerated." Rick had to call the executives of the milk company, and they agreed.

Rick made another decision. He called the local radio station, which by Tuesday was the Cape's only link with the world. The station was into full hurricane coverage. It was so detailed, in fact, that hardly anybody in Falmouth knew anything about the short-lived coup in the Soviet Union, which was occurring the same week. So Rick told the station that he had a milk truck in his lot. The station, ignoring the Soviet coup, told its listeners about the Kenyon's milk truck numerous times on Tuesday. It was yet another coup—a public relations coup.

Tuesday was even busier than Monday. In a crisis, with most competitors shut down and losing perishables, Rick LeMoine flourished. Sure, Rick lost some goods too. But not half of what he could have lost if he hadn't made some quick decisions. And even with some of the losses—for example, the ice cream—the image of the store profited. And the tills of the store profited too—it was the most profitable two days in the history of the store. Rick showed why, especially in crisis, any decision is better than no decision.

Three days after the hurricane some men from the power company were working near Kenyon's to get the power restored. As it turned out, some areas of the Cape lost power for seven days. But it was not to be for Rick. He walked out to talk to the men, who were packing up to go elsewhere. There was still no power at Kenyon's. "Where are you going?" asked Rick.

To another part of town, he was told. They had been called by management. There was something more urgent.

"But how long would it take to get power on at Kenyon's?" he asked.

About a half hour, he was told. They started to walk to the truck.

"How about a case of beer for each man if you do it now?" he asked. Rick pleaded his case. Ten minutes later the power at Kenyon's was on, and he gave each of them a case of beer.

The first thing Rick did after that was drive to his partner's store to loan him the generator.

Vapor lock is caused by fear. Fear of failure. Fear of the unknown. Fear of the known. But decisiveness is the mark of a leader. By creating action where there is inaction, a leader leads rather than wallows. A leader radiates confidence, and confidence is decisive.

There is a saying: Lead, follow, or get out of the way. It's a good saying. Make a decision. What's it going to be—yes or no? Even worse than the word "no" is no decision. Leaders need to say "yes" more, but even a "no," if done quickly, can be a motivator. The absence of decision is always negative—it reeks of fear.

Goethe said, "What you can do, or dream you can, begin it. Boldness has a genius, power, and magic in it." Boldness. Urgency. You cannot take 1,000 steps without taking the first one.

Fear of failure is in essence fear of risk. John Lennon wrote, "Life is what happens when you're busy making other plans." If you are always planning, you are never doing. At some point you have to jump.

In some things, especially in the realm of adventuring, risk can appear to be no more than educated lunacy. Climbing Mt. Everest, for instance, may seem so, but climbers know what they're doing. It's still risky, but if the spark of genius hits you and you have tested it, you have to follow it.

Or you have to let it go and move on to something else. One of the two—no middle ground.

The anxiety and agitation of tense muscles and even tenser brain tissue can only hold for so long. At some point with indecision it all explodes, and you cease being human with human emotions.

The consequence of indecision can be enormous. Worst of all, it is not a sudden catastrophe but rather a slow death, decades of misery contemplating what might have been, like the punch-drunk ex-fighter continually claiming, "I coulda been a contender."

Dugald Stermer could have been that way. Stermer is a world-renowned illustrator—a one-man award-winning, politically influential artist. He has illustrated literally hundreds of editorial and advertising pages, including *Time* magazine covers, environmental posters, and the 1984 Olympic medals. When he was a young man at a career crossroad, Stermer didn't hesitate. He didn't have any example, any paradigm; he just followed his instinct. He figured he could create his own career path, one to make him happy.

He was attending art school, but art school for Stermer was too restrictive. He once said, "I would feel very uncomfortable if there wasn't political or editorial content in much of my work." So he quit art school and moved on to UCLA, where he meshed his political and artistic instincts into a freelance career as designer, illustrator, and writer. He made a decision and he jumped. There were times when it was all a maddening struggle with periods of grave uncertainty. But he made up his mind and forged ahead, convinced his quest was correct.

Stermer aims to educate. His latest books have dealt with extinction of plants and animals. Before his book

Vanishing Flora came out he said, "Most of what we know about medicine, nutrition, and food has been derived from plants. And sadly, by the time the book comes out, 15 or 30 of the flowers in it will be extinct. We're losing up to three species a day . . . even as the Amazon rain forest is destroyed. Gone before we've even had a chance to identify or to ever understand their qualities.

"The lesson is, finally, that a species may disappear from the earth, but it leaves behind an ecological void forever, and too often the man-made causes for its extinction also remain . . . a threat to every other living creature . . . including ourselves."

If Stermer had not been strong enough to make a decision and stick with it, he might never have been able to work toward preserving nature, his passion. That would have been sad. The world would have been a lesser place for it. After all, as noted above, Stermer is no mere illustrator—he is a historian, recording our world as it may never be again.

You have to go at a goal like a fish attacks a fish ladder—one step at a time, without discouragement. You must have an inner confidence in order to radiate it, because expectation of failure almost guarantees it.

It happened to Karl Wallenda, patriarch of the great tightrope-walking family. For years and years his act was incredibly successful—he toured the world and thrilled thousands with his daring. But then one day something happened. Wallenda, before he was due to walk the high wire, became edgy. He wanted to know the wind currents, and he checked the wire himself—something he rarely did. He checked over and over. He was wary.

It was a time he should have said no. He should have realized what was wrong with his mental makeup that day.

For the first time ever he lacked confidence. That day, Karl Wallenda fell to his death.

Unless you are undertaking a life-threatening adventure like Karl Wallenda, the world doesn't end with failure. Rather, lessons are learned. Failure is often the inability to properly assess risk. What comes from failure is an education. A leader learns where the error was and doesn't make it again. If you are not deterred by the loss, you will be smarter and more efficient.

The people who are afraid of failure just don't get it. Failure is closer to success than it is to mediocrity. Failure isn't bad; it's good. It shouldn't crush; it should inspire. Easy words, I know, but none are more true. Every great person has experienced failure in some fashion. It is the mark of a great person to be able to deal with failure—it often leads to success.

The great thing about coming out of failure is that you learn about yourself in ways that no other experience can teach. You learn about resilience and survival. Risk becomes easier. You are smarter and better able to assess risk. You have a depth of knowledge about your toughness in crisis. To go again and again is the key to your success—both as an individual and as a leader.

David Lloyd George said, "Don't be afraid to take a big step when one is indicated. You can't cross a chasm in two small jumps." Although it is never wise to make decisions blindly, it is also true that risk-averse pensiveness is often the riskiest of all actions.

Boeing proved the wisdom of a quick decision in a crisis following the crash of a Japan Airlines jet into a mountain in Japan. It was a horrible tragedy—hundreds of Japanese citizens died. Two days after the wreck the president of Boeing claimed full responsibility for the crash. In America this would have been a major mistake—the normal way in such tragedies is to let the courts decide responsibility. But the president of Boeing knew Japanese culture was much different. He knew about leadership. Despite his lawyer's advice the president of Boeing took full responsibility, in the media, without the benefits of a full inquiry. The crash could have been the pilot's fault, or a result of wind shear or any number of possible causes. But Boeing took responsibility, and the Japanese respected that. It was honorable, and it was clear that Boeing was run by responsible leadership. Weeks later Boeing sold hundreds of millions of dollars worth of planes to another airline based in Japan. That airline had seen and approved of Boeing's actions.

An opposite example is Exxon's handling of the Exxon Valdez crisis, in which their tanker hit an iceberg and spilled millions of gallons of oil into pristine Prince William Sound in Alaska. Exxon followed the classic MBA-lawyer approach to crisis. Deny everything. Duck responsibility. Hope it will go away and talk about a historical success record. They hired a public relations firm from Houston to talk to the media, but the PR people didn't even visit Alaska until more than two weeks after the spill. The PR people chose to stay in their offices in Houston issuing communiqués trying to logically explain away the undermanned, single-hulled tankers Exxon was using, despite Exxon's being continually urged to upgrade their staff and to use stronger ships.

To justify its efforts in Alaska, Exxon had paid lip service to the concept of being a leader in conservation and environmental issues. At a time when Exxon was showing what many described as obscene profits, it severely tarnished its image by not even sending a high-ranking representative to Alaska to show it cared. Exxon just waited for things to play out rather than make a quick decision. It was the classic ostrich mentality—head in the sand.

A quick decision in the Exxon Valdez case would certainly have helped. Granted, it was a no-win situation. But rather than wait and run from responsibility, Exxon should have moved forward to accept it and be the leader—even if it was in the cleanup process. Instead the company waited for the courts to dictate and to impose the cost of the spill. When anyone pays after being ordered to do so by a court, no one gives them any credit. People see them as only paying after being dragged kicking and screaming into court. Crisis is an opportunity to display leadership or shirk from it.

A decision is a wonderful thing because it implies action. Even if a decision is no, it can be a positive force because it means a leader is confident in his abilities.

Risk aversion is all about failure and fear of failure. One major cause of failure is expectation of failure. Conversely, one major cause of success is the expectation of such.

Positive visualizion works. It has been proven. Professional athletes universally rely on visualization for improving technique. Even medical patients have found attitude a key ingredient to improving their health.

In a study of basketball free-throw shooters the players were divided equally, based on talent, into three groups. One group shot zero free throws for a month. The second group shot 50 free throws a day for a month. The third group visualized shooting 50 perfect free throws every day for a month.

At the end of the month the three groups had a shoot off. The lowest score was posted by those who didn't practice. The highest was by the group doing the visualization. The lesson is clear: the group visualizing the perfect shots did not have the negative feedback of the practicing group (the group practicing missed a lot of shots). As a result the group doing the visualizing had a more positive attitude and better results.

In reality, of course, it was not a group that was visualizing, but individuals. Decisions that motivate are always made by individuals. Individuals can make quick decisions. Committees, on the other hand, are by their nature stifling. They operate on the basis of consensus building in a world of compromise and institutional memory. Individuality is lost to the greater good of the group, and self-interests are beholden to others for potential future assistance. As time goes on the committee mentality intensifies and a risk-averse paralysis sets in.

Just look at government—a world of committees. The backslapping and consensus building that often may be necessary to run a government is one reason very little ever gets done. There is always an unspoken fear that someone may have to take responsibility for a failure, and so no one tries anything.

It is the same in business. If a committee is set up, it should have a sunset provision in its charter—mandating its extinction at a certain, set time. If a committee is not set up with a specific purpose in mind, its goal soon becomes preservation of the committee. And committees stifle decisiveness.

The reason committees stifle decisiveness is because they overpower individuality, and thus audacity. If there is a strong leader, unimpeded by a committee, the audacity to make strong decisions will filter down into the rest of the company. Audacity in hiring, decision making, and especially in goal setting is inspiring internally and can frequently be the difference between two firms competing for the same customer. A strong decision is one in which the individual making it believes in his or her own strength of character as a force that will not be stopped.

In 1975, The North Face was faced with an enormous problem that I could have easily ignored and blamed on outside forces. The quality and quantity of goose down in the market was below the standards acceptable to us. As availability dried up, importers and middlemen began to "cut" the product by inserting dust, feathers, used down, and anything else that would increase the weight. (Down is sold on the basis of weight.)

By this time our reputation for making the best had been established. Much of our quality and leadership image was predicated on our goose down jackets—the best in the world. If we went along with what the goose down market offered, it would destroy that image and in essence kill the company.

It was time to jump off the fence. I had to do something. Some suggested capitulating to the market conditions. Some suggested forming a committee to study the problem.

But I jumped farther, as far as I could. I decided to visit the People's Republic of China. That country represented 60 percent of the world's raw goose down market. Some people even said it was 80 percent. In China the down was sold to middlemen from around the world who then processed it and sold it to manufacturers such as ourselves. But as I said, the middlemen were "cutting" it to give them higher profits and false levels of success. It was a major problem.

There was another problem. It was shortly after President Nixon first visited China. After 25 years of the two countries' arguing, hardly anyone was going from the United States to China, and doing business with China was very complex—requiring the use of intermediary banks and antiquated communication systems. At one point China would not even honor traveler's check from the United States. Doing business with China took audacity—it was a battle with decades of political and cultural ill will behind it. My audacity was one born of desperation.

It also took flexibility. I couldn't accomplish this on my own. I needed help, someone who knew about China. Enter Frank Chang, a friend of one of the 60 or so Chinese employees at The North Face. "Give me your passport and I'll get you an invitation," Chang said. "I'll send the invitation along with your passport to Washington, and you'll get a visa." I was wary. It was my passport—a most valuable item. But this was an opportunity. I jumped.

Three weeks later one of my vice presidents and I were on our way to Canton, China. We were on a mission to buy Chinese goose down and save the company.

I knew virtually nothing of the worldwide goose down market. I didn't have much need to—until the opportunity to go to China arose. Before the trip I began to ask around. And I took out some books on the goose down industry from the library. Airplane reading—this was not so much a jump as a free-fall into a decision. Our hand was forced, since to do nothing would be to fail.

We had heard China didn't have enough down for the world market and therefore would sell only to "old friends." We weren't old friends. We weren't even friends. Not yet, anyway.

There were other problems. Processing down is a cumbersome procedure that requires lots of machinery and space. The machinery is expensive, and the space is needed to handle the voluminous nature of the down. Purchasing directly meant we would be competing with our suppliers—a potentially touchy situation. Finally we estimated it would cost more than $100,000—a significant chunk of our cash flow—to buy the down we needed. This was not going to be easy, but the alternative of lower quality was absolutely unacceptable.

I made a decision, and off we went on another adventure. I started out logically. I analyzed the problems, and our sales pitch, on the plane to China. Our legitimate need for down was a selling point, even though we were not old friends. I knew that if our suppliers were so greedy as to debase the product for profit, they would probably also process it for us—even though they didn't like our competition. I knew I could come up with the cash because the market demand was greatly exceeding supply, so retail prices would surely go up. The investment made so much sense that I was convinced even our bankers would agree.

The Canton Trade Fair was incredible—a huge fairgrounds of socialistic celebration. There were tremendous pictures of Mao and Chou En-lai hung everywhere. Martial music played continually on the outdoor speakers. It was ungodly hot in this city on the Pearl River—90 degrees Farenheit and 90 percent humidity.

We stayed in the Tung Fang Hotel, a clean, spartan establishment famous for its proximity to the Canton Trade Fair; its mosquito netting over the beds; and the steel-wool, rough blankets on top of them. On the only table in my room there was a large rotating fan—"the people's fan," we called it. The room had all the comforts of modern Chinese technology; there were no capitalistic excesses.

The first night, after an exotic and excessive dinner, we went to the top floor of the hotel—a nightclub of sorts. It was very strange, not like any nightclub we had ever seen. There was bare neon tube lighting in a stark, cement-walled room. Humidity ran down the walls and in some places formed puddles on the floor. There were people from everywhere, of every commercial persuasion, though most were from the socialist part of the world. At one point, like a scene from a grainy black-and-white film, two apparent Arabs in long, flowing robes got into an argument. They wrestled each other to the floor, rolling in the muddy water. It was utterly comical, quite disorienting, and an unsettling prelude to the negotiations for Chinese goose down.

The next morning was just as comical. When we got to the fair, we had to go to a starting line, which all who weren't "old friends" had to do before the fair began. In an egalitarian, socialistic way meetings for newcomers were truly on a first-come, first-serve basis.

We got to the starting line first. A ribbon was strung across it. The day was already hot, and it was damp and slippery. People began to crowd around us and the martial music played on, with the pictures of Mao and Chou En-lai sitting in approval. The bell signaling the start of the fair sounded. The ribbon in front of us dropped, and everyone started running. We did. We laughed too, for this was almost slapstick—a United Nations' representation practically, and we were all running in our native dress for the opportunity to buy Chinese exports.

When the bell had sounded, some people just out of the starting gate fell on the slippery, muddy floor. But we survived—through force of will and lots of luck. I presume it was also our American athletic prowess. We were the first to arrive at the Animal By-product Import and Export Corporation, the one that sold all the down. They had a monopoly. We arrived in dark suits, dripping wet from our mad dash in the heat and looking nothing like international business leaders. Still, I was really charged up.

At the table, there were three of us—my vice president, our translator, and myself. And fourteen of them. They were all dressed alike in ill-fitting blue jackets and white shirts, all except the head of the delegation, who appeared to have a better tailor, though the same blue jacket and white shirt. The outfit appeared to be a Chinese version of the American business suit. Conformity has no cultural bounds—there's embalming fluid everywhere.

The head of the committee stared at me. He asked me to explain to him the world goose down market. He gave off an air of fraudulent authority, that he was better than me by virtue of his power. He tested me.

"You know better than I, but if you want my version, I'll be glad to tell you," I said. I gave him facts. I gave him figures. And I told him how the middlemen were destroying the quality image of China by cutting the down.

"You are wrong," he said. "Wrong, wrong, wrong."

He looked at us in silence. His comrades did too.

I decided to jump once again. "You say no," I repeated. I looked him right in the eye as I said the words I knew he needed translated. "But my research and experience tells me what I'm saying is true." I called his bluff. I knew, or at least I thought I knew, that my facts were correct. I really didn't have another choice.

He smiled a wry smile. I looked across the table to a man next to him. That person was busy writing. I looked again. He was copying my notes, in English, upside down from across the table. It was incredible—this man had never spoken any English or even indicated any knowledge of my language.

The head of the delegation told us there was no down for sale. My heart sank. I was on the other side of the world and my worst nightmare was happening—I was failing in my quest. Our company was threatened. My employees were threatened.

I did the only thing left to do. I started talking, and so did my vice president. We went into overdrive—holding out our naked spark for them all to see.

"We're not here to exploit China," I said. "We are valid users. It's the middlemen who are dishonest. You know, the ones you've been selling to. We want to maintain quality. We are good for China's image. The middlemen are harming your image. I had to come here to tell you this and make something different happen.

"Don't you see?" I asked. "We are your friends in America. We have 60 loyal Chinese workers. One of them helped me to come here. If you turn me down, they will be out of a job, we will be out of business, and you will have missed the best long-term opportunity you'll see in a long time. We're here to give you flexibility and to establish a long-term relationship."

I finished. I looked at him—I was raw nerve at that moment. Fully exposed with sensation to the core of my existence.

"Come back tomorrow," he said.

The next day he asked how much down we wanted. I said, "We need five metric tons. That's how much we need to keep the factory running." It all seemed to be going better. Perhaps we had passed his test.

He asked if we would sell to others. We said no. We just wanted the quality and quantity that we needed for our own factory. He told us to come back tomorrow—maybe, just maybe we would have a contract.

We were overjoyed. The next day he did indeed have a contract for us. But instead of five tons, it was for 500 tons. We could not possibly use 500 tons. To use that much we would have to sell it all over the world. It was way beyond our needs. My mind started spinning. We didn't have the facilities to store even five tons—never 500 tons. If we were to buy the down and resell it, we would have to be dishonest with the Chinese, whom we had told we did not intend to sell the down. Financing was a third issue. Now we were talking about millions of dollars, not $100,000. And finally, we would have to change the nature of our business from a high-quality goose down clothing manufacturer to that of a middleman in the market.

There was a good side, a huge good side. The market for down was sure to double in price due to the shortage, and we would get rich in six months.

I jumped again. I said no. "I think a mistake has been made," I said. "We only need five tons for our factory."

He smiled his wry smile again. He apologized and promised to rewrite the contract.

It was rewritten, we got the down, and our quality image prospered. Many of our competitors did not. When it was time to jump off the fence and make a decision, the competition waited to see what would happen.

When they ended up with lower-quality down, some lowered the quality of their products and told their customers. Others lowered their quality and didn't tell their customers. By then, any decision for them was a bad one. The honest companies suffered because of their lower quality goods. The dishonest ones suffered more. The government investigated many of those companies and filed actions against those that didn't comply with government standards.

Decisions are not always easy, but the returns are constant—immediate feedback, more opportunities, and a greater camaraderie. When it is time, when you know what you stand for and what your vision is, you might as well jump. Take a risk; you won't regret it.

Risk is exactly what it says, a chance. Each challenge accepted should be a hypothesis based on two things: ability and desire. You must have the ability and the desire to accomplish something. Without both, risk is folly.

There is more to it than blindly and endlessly throwing your body into the wind tunnel of risk. You must continually assess your goals and means of reaching them. You must have an absolute inner confidence that you can continually tap. The spark is always your strength—find it and jump.

6

Starting in the Warehouse:

Every Decision Is a Statement

After I didn't get hired by General Mills, General Electric, and General Motors, I went to work as general manager of a company in Berkeley called The Ski Hut. It was my first adult job—post-MBA, pre-The North Face.

The Ski Hut was involved in something I liked—hiking and backpacking—and it was an opportunity to grow in a job that would challenge me. Not only that, the owner told me if I turned his business around, I could buy it. So in I came, Johnny-with-an-MBA, all set to turn around The Ski Hut.

Everybody eyed me suspiciously. There were about 25

employees, and the first assumption was that I would fire them all and replace them with my own people. I could sense the tension, and I was the focus of it. I could feel every movement of mine getting scrutinized. I could almost see the muscles in everyone's neck tighten whenever I walked into a room.

Because I had an MBA, everybody thought The Ski Hut would soon become a suit-and-tie establishment with management by manipulation. Fear was apparently a driving force in this company. Most people seemed guided by their personal motivations, with no company orientation whatsoever. They were just scared, and I, as the new boss, was just another unknown to fear.

It was not a good situation, and neither were the financials. I had been hired to turn the company around. A cursory look at the numbers revealed two things: the results were abysmal, yet it was impossible to find the cause. The numbers didn't tell the story.

It seemed, from an MBA, theoretical standpoint, that it would make sense to delve into the financial status of the company a lot further before jumping into the maelstrom of human emotions that created those depressing numbers.

But I knew business was about more than numbers. And I knew how important my actions were, especially at the beginning.

The first week was the typical awkward period. An opening night is always difficult. We put our little feelers out, trying to get to know each other. I walked around introducing myself, trying to put people at ease. I looked them in the eye. I smiled and I meant it. I asked questions, and I took an interest in the opinions of the employees.

Contrary to popular opinion, I had no intention of firing anyone, I explained. I wanted to find out how the company worked—who did what, when, and how. I also explained that my goal was to make The Ski Hut successful—not just for the owner's benefit, but for everyone's. I wanted to learn about the people who were now my employees. I wanted to know more than just how they did their job. It was important that I showed I cared, because I genuinely did. What I learned through this process was that 24 of the 25 employees were great and well suited to their jobs. One, however, had to be fired.

He was the warehouse manager and a nice person, but not particularly into his job. He had an idiosyncrasy that kept him from doing some of the work. He was a believer in Meher Baba, the religious leader. I am an open person—believe what you want, I thought. But then I learned a bit more about this religion. Apparently Meher Baba doesn't speak. And so on Meher Baba's birthday, all his followers won't speak either.

Wouldn't you know it, on my first week on the job it was Meher Baba's birthday and we had a number of shipments scheduled to go out. A major part of a warehouse manager's job required verbal communication. Silence doesn't cut it on the day of a shipment—it requires constant interaction. When I pointed this out to the warehouse manager, he stood looking at me like I was some money-grubbing blasphemer. He refused to work. Of course, he didn't tell me this. He wrote a note.

I really had no problem with his religion. It's just that some people have the wrong jobs, and our warehouse manager was one of them. You can be what you want to be—a Meher Baba believer, if you want. But first you have to do your job. The key is to have a job that fits your beliefs. The demands of the job of a warehouse manager obviously didn't fit this person. His life was out of tune.

My action, I knew, would cause a stir. That was the idea. Everything I did that first week was magnified. Everything I did was a statement about myself and my vision of the company.

I walked around and looked at the physical orientation of the facility. Right outside the office was a warehouse. Nothing was in order. Everything was stacked on top of everything else. It was organizational chaos. The books needed as much organizing as the warehouse; without that it was impossible to understand the flow of money and inventory. But the warehouse had to come first. We were missing sales because it was difficult and sometimes impossible to find the products in it.

I made a decision. I spent two days in the warehouse. I got sweaty and dirty with everyone else, and we physically reorganized the warehouse so it was easy to access and stock. I knew early on I had to set an example of my way, and the best example was a visual one—everybody could see it. My actions showed many things: I wasn't afraid of work; satisfying the customer was key; I believed in organization and efficiency; and most important, I knew there was no bottom line without a top line—we needed sales to make a profit.

I could have reorganized the books, but no one would have seen it. What good would that do morale? None—except, perhaps, for that of one sun-allergic accountant wringing his hands gleefully, alone in a corner cubicle with a calculator and spread sheets.

I could have given a speech or written memos. But who would really care? Actions always speak louder than words because business is about action, not empty promises or threats. People sensed that I cared by my efforts to get to know them. They knew I was serious by my firing of the warehouse manager. And they found out I knew how business really works by my concentration on the warehouse before the books. I made my mark in that first week. The troops rallied around, and we worked together toward mutual goals.

But a year later, after we had turned The Ski Hut around and I wasn't needed any longer, the owner refused to live up to his promise to sell the company to me. So I did something symbolic at that point too. I quit.

Quitting may be the ultimate symbolic act of business. It is, of course, more than symbolic. It's personal. And that's the point. Symbolism without depth is empty sloganeering. The reason for the symbolic act is not Machiavellian. It is humanistic. It is designed to touch the soul—to inspire as the wind does a bird.

Every decision is a statement, even those decisions you don't intend as such. Some are statements to the masses. Some are statements to a few. All are statements to and about yourself.

When Stephen Wolf was hired to be CEO of Flying Tiger Airlines, his job was simple: Turn it around. When he came to the job, he was told a lot had to be done—fast. The company's finances were less than perfect, the organization was in disarray, and the energy level and commitment of employees was abysmal. In many ways it looked to be a dying company—numb, failing, and bored.

Wolf knew he had to act fast and his actions had to be visible—something that spoke to the heart of his people as well as their minds. He had to do what most in the company felt management would never do—sell "the yacht" and fire Pierre. It was that drastic.

"The yacht," as most in the company called her, was a 40-foot cruiser. It was on a mooring in Marina del Rey,

California. Wolf said the company would also give up the ship's mooring. In reality the savings from these two moves were minimal. The boat was paid for, and the cost of maintaining it was a trifle compared to the maintenance of such things as the Flying Tiger airplanes. The mooring cost was also financially not very significant because of a long-term, sweetheart deal signed years before. But getting rid of the icons signaled to workers that the problem was serious. The executives were cutting down; everyone should.

At the same time that he sold the boat, Wolf closed the executive dining room and fired the chef, Pierre. He was cutting fat, and he wanted everyone to know it. These actions were more symbolic than effectual changes—on the surface. But the deeper reality was that he often gave speeches and talked privately to employees. Always he would remind people how he "sold the yacht and fired Pierre." It was great symbolism—especially the name "Pierre"—because it conjured up images of expensive and exotic French meals. The message was clear—the only thing sacred was the mission to make the company healthy.

Wolf didn't stop there. He was an incredibly hard worker, and he made sure everyone knew it—first to arrive, last to leave. The idea was to change the work ethic. He stood for hard work. His car was well known to employees. He always parked by the door so everyone could see he was there when they came, and when they left.

Hard work was his standard. He established what he called a chairman's conference. For weeks at a time he would fly to the far reaches of the world to explain to employees of Flying Tiger the need for the turnaround—the urgency. His schedule was posted on bulletin boards throughout the company. Everyone followed his exhaustive itinerary. It was obvious to anyone who looked that the only time he had to sleep was on the airplane between destinations. The message was always urgency and hard work.

He even made a statement to the stockholders by his actions. He accepted a compensation package that had only a modest cash salary, but significant stock options—symbolic of his long-term belief in the company and himself.

Wolf is a leader, not just a manager. There is a huge difference. Managers produce and direct. Leaders understand the implications, ramifications, and complications of their actions. Managers work with organization charts and job descriptions. Leaders work with dreams and defeats. Managers understand pie charts, bar graphs, and punctuation. Leaders do too. But leaders know more. Leaders know caring, passion, and poetry. Leaders know people.

Although it may appear in some companies that a leader's principal job is to shuffle papers and referee disputes, this simply is not true. The reality of the job is that greatness comes only when others accomplish great things. The biggest spark in the world without support is just a spark—it will die out.

Paper shuffling may thrill a few, but it won't excite the masses. It will, however, make a statement—that paper is more important than people. Every action makes a statement about priorities. The priority of a leader, quite simply, is to lead. If the statement says otherwise, there is a void of leadership.

It is essential for a leader to understand the significance of his or her actions—to realize that those symbols affect people on a very human level. Symbolism communicates.

A leader has to get across the message that this is more than just a job—it is an integral part of life. The human connections are the key.

At The North Face, whenever we moved into a new building, we would have a painting party. For one thing, it saved money if we painted the building ourselves. But more importantly, it allowed all of us to work side by side for a day or two. It broke down the hierarchy. It told people we were all equal, we just had different jobs. And it allowed some in the office staff, such as myself, to realize the quality of workers we had on the maintenance staff, who were definitely better than we were at the task of painting.

At one painting party, I was up on some scaffolding and happened to be working next to the newest employee in the company, Bob Lutz. It was his first day. We worked side by side for about two hours, exchanging small talk and working hard helping each other. Eventually, Bob asked what I did for The North Face. I didn't want to blurt out "president." Instead I tried to describe my various duties. I thought I did a good job explaining it all, but Bob just looked baffled. I went on, telling him as best I could about all the abstract duties I felt were mine. Finally, while we were moving the scaffolding, he looked at me and said, "Gosh, it doesn't sound like you're very busy."

Pride got the best of me at that point and I told him I was president. He was embarrassed for having made light of my job. But I was humored. On the surface, I supposed, he was right. We talked more. I explained to him how simply showing up and working at a painting party was one of the most important parts of my job. I connected with Bob that day. From then on, we were always able to talk.

A direct relationship, like mine with Bob, is the ideal. Symbolism and vision are never lost because the connection is so direct. But as a company grows, it becomes impossible to deal directly with every individual. A transformation takes place at some point in a company's growth, and it takes an astute individual to recognize and adjust to the changes. To adapt is to lead.

Still, the inspiration of the individual is always the ultimate goal. Always. A human spirit is an entity unto itself with potential so enormous it boggles the mind. Humans want to be inspired. Every person desires greatness, and a leader taps into that desire. But as the transformation from a small to a large company takes place, a leader must also make changes, adjusting from an individual approach to one that is broader but no less personal. The goal is always to inspire.

People want to be led; they want a vision to follow. In large organizations in order for people to know what a leader is about they look at his or her actions. An astute leader acts accordingly.

You have to walk the walk and talk the talk. It can't be an act, because soon it will be transparent as such. People don't follow hypocrites. I reiterate: every decision makes a statement. Every action. You cannot be selective about what others see—life happens, and people watch.

A man who made apparel for the ski industry learned this lesson too late. Before getting into apparel with his company, he was a world ski champion. Moving into ski apparel seemed a natural progression for him. But some of the qualities that made him a good racer—ego, focus on self—turned out to be his downfall.

His problem was the way he treated people. The symbolism of his acts conveyed the message that he was not a man to be trusted. As a result whenever anyone had a choice, that person didn't want to deal with him.

He was the same way with his dealers. In an interview in a major ski publication he carefully explained how there were only four smart people in the entire ski business. This man, of course, was one of the four. When his ski wear was no longer "hot," it was all the "dumb" people who refused to buy from him.

His most famous gaffe came after one of his best sales representatives died. Prior to that, this owner had already had a reputation for treating his reps poorly. Whenever they disagreed, he fired them. When the reps gave advice, he turned away. He always knew best—he was one of the four "smart" people, after all. Just before the sales rep died, he had written some new orders. But obviously he couldn't get back out to follow up. The owner of the company had to hire someone to take his place. Clearly the rule in sales is the person who writes the order gets the commission. But the owner refused to pay the salesman's widow the commissions. His reasoning, I guess, was that he also had to pay the new salesman to go out and follow up on the orders. He was callous and cold. He didn't care about people, only about himself.

Due to his designs and innovation, he was, for a while, on the top of the ski apparel business. Eventually people realized that even his brilliance for design couldn't overcome his leadership shortcomings. He couldn't hold on to good people, and his personal strengths—as good as they were—were not enough to sustain the company. The company faltered. When he tried to get others to help him out, no one would. In business, you see the same people on the way down who you saw on the way up. People remember.

The Man Who Skied Down Everest is a 1970 film about a Japanese skier whose goal it was to ski down the highest peak in the world. The film shows him skiing down a short way, doing a few classic jump turns, and then falling a tremendous length. He had a parachute that dragged behind him and finally stopped his fall, a few feet short of a crevasse and certain death. Friends of mine jokingly refer to him as "the man who fell down Everest."

What the film didn't capture, however, was the way the Japanese skier, Yuichiro Miura, abused all around him to meet his goal. The overall crew was 34 people, including 10 cameramen and 27 tons of goods. To ski down Everest, first Miura had to climb it. He put together a team of Sherpas for support, but he refused to listen to them. He thought that by using the film, he came across as a man of character and courage. The reality is much different. While climbing, the crew came to an ice fall, and the Sherpas warned Miura it was dangerous to go forward. The Sherpas have a mystical, metaphysical relationship with the mountains—they respect them as living deities. They do not force their will on a mountain. They knew the ice was moving, and even though it appeared safe, it could quickly become perilous. Miura would hear none of it—he felt he had to press on. He berated the Sherpas. He told them he knew what was right. The only thing that matters, he said in essence, is my goal.

Without the Sherpas, the climb could not have proceeded. But they needed the money, and so they accepted Miura's demands. In the midst of the ice fall there was a disaster—six Sherpas died. The leader of the Sherpas was wild with indignation and tried to kill Miura with an ice ax for driving the others to their death. To Miura, though, the accident was inconsequential, because he could still reach his goal. He put together the remains of the team and made it up the mountain to the point where he could begin his descent. He made his film.

The man who skied down Everest, like the ski apparel executive, failed to recognize the human connections that are needed for true success. The negative symbolism they put forth to all around them made what successes they did have hollow.

It is easy to recognize negative symbolism because people expect to be treated as human beings, and when they aren't, it stands out.

Successful symbols are often more difficult to describe because success is the result of many things. Failure can be the result of one major act. The symbolism most people take for granted is positive. People expect others to be honest. They expect to be treated fairly. They even expect companies to be successful. This does not diminish the importance of positive symbolic acts. It is important to ratify people's expectations.

One of the goals in any business is to have a happy and productive work force. Again, this comes back to people's expectations. If you meet those expectations, you go a long way toward ensuring that people are happy and productive.

Even Stephen Wolf, well versed in symbolism, made a slip—a big slip. Wolf is now CEO of United Airlines. Shortly after taking that job, he presented a leveraged buy-out proposal to the board as a means of helping solve the airline's problems. But when the media reported it, the thing employees noticed most was that Wolf stood to make $70 million on the deal. The workers were also part of the buy out, but it was predicated on asking the workers to make concessions to allow the deal to work. Workers were outraged at being asked to make concessions so that Wolf could make $70 million. Of course, it wasn't that simple, but the workers saw it that way. The buy out didn't go through. For a while Wolf and the workers weren't talking. Finally there was rapprochement, and the offer was restructured so that Wolf still made a good amount of money, but nowhere near $70 million. He took control of United and has been quite successful. But his story illustrates that even an apparent master of symbolism can be seriously hurt by one bad action.

What you do tells people about what you think. A closed door may provide an opportunity for extra work, but it also telegraphs the message that some things are secret and visitors are not welcome. Limited access to information on computers sends the same message.

The upkeep of your facility tells a lot about the quality of your products and your attention to detail. Things such as clean trucks, pruned gardens, and painted buildings, though not essential on one level, are really symbols of how much you care about your employees, your customers, and your product. A child-care facility, for instance, says as much to your employees about how you care for them as human beings as does their paycheck.

Two symbols—promotions and money—are generally the most important internal symbols. If you promote on the basis of tenure rather than talent, it tells those with talent that skill has nothing to do with advancement.

Compensation is probably the strongest symbol. If inequities exist, the workers will know. In one company I've worked with, the owner devised a complex system to calculate Christmas bonuses. The system was based on years of service, salary, a subjective judgment of how hard people worked, and about four other items. It was absurd—a rationalization to screw people. The formula was skewed so much to the owner that he received 93 percent of the bonus—the other 24 people split the remaining 7 percent. He thought that because he made it so formal, everyone would think it was fair. The reality was everyone thought he was trying to dupe them. Ducking reality, the owner asked one of his underlings to hand out the bonuses. Another employee in a fit of pique handed back his $25 bonus because, in his words, "the owner obviously needs it more than me."

Two other symbols—set up specifically to be symbols—are important enough to highlight. One is a mission statement. Unfortunately most mission statements don't work because they are written by committees and read like it. They are long, they cover every contingency, and they are impossible to memorize. The best mission statements are the shortest. It has to be easy to memorize, and one that employees can state verbally with pride. Perhaps the best ever is IBM's: "Think." It isn't specific, but it covers everything.

The other obvious symbol is the selection of a company logo—it becomes a clear symbol of what you are. A low-cost, price-oriented company must have a symbol that is simple, clean, and frugal. A company selling high-cost, fashion-oriented items must have something that puts that image across. When you present your business card to a Japanese, you will see that person scrutinize it for much longer than an American would. They believe that what you stand for is represented by the graphic on your card. It is often the first impression you make on your customer—its importance transcends its cost.

But for all that logos and mission statements say about a company on first glance, it is the actions of a company over the long haul that make the most important statement. Individual statements have a definitive life span. You cannot do one symbolic act and then assume it will last forever. You must continually do the symbolic, and always understand that everything you do has symbolic implications. Life is fluid; views change.

In 1982, The North Face acquired a manufacturing firm, Black's of Greenock, in Scotland. The idea was to provide a local manufacturing base to service our European dealers from inside the European Common Market. Black's was a venerable name. The company had started with sails for clipper ships and evolved into manufacturing outdoor clothing and products.

But Black's had fallen on hard times. In an effort to cut costs, it virtually stopped new product design and marketing. The inevitable happened—lower sales. They cut costs again, which led to even lower sales.

When we arrived, the work force was 70 percent less than at Black's peak. People were demoralized and paranoid about their future.

I assigned Bob Gorton, manager of one of our retail divisions, to be managing director in Scotland. His enthusiasm for the position was infectious, and his track record at The North Face was superb.

We began by discussing how to run the company: like a typical British firm with hierarchy and formality, or in the more casual way we ran The North Face in Berkeley. The decision was easy. We opted to bring the Berkeley way to Scotland. It reflected our personality.

A leader's style creates the foundation for the team. I've seen autocrats and delegators develop great teams. The most important factor was that the leaders were genuine. I prefer to delegate, but the key is for employees to know who you are. You have to show them *you*, not a cardboard cutout that spins in the wind.

On the day we signed the final papers, Bob and I met with all the workers and explained our vision, our demand to be the best, and our personal dedication to success in Scotland. We also explained our open-door policy to the executive offices. This was no mere change in policy; it was revolution. The workers were skeptical. Under the old regime the only time the workers had gone into the executive offices was if their names were called over the loudspeaker. "Come to the offices" meant to them "You are about to be fired." That day as I was addressing the employees, one of the seamstresses turned to another and I overheard her say, "Let's wait a couple of weeks and see if the cowboys from the Colonies are still talking to us."

We were, and they loved it! Bob became one of the most popular people in the company. When he resigned eight years later to join me on my consulting projects, people were openly sad and emotional. His humanistic approach had touched their hearts.

But not all was smooth sailing. Some workers simply could not adjust to our open ways. A few months after we took over Black's, I was back in Scotland. The head of the sales force (a sales force, by the way, that we were obligated to use for one year as part of the acquisition agreement) pulled me aside for what he called "a personal discussion."

"You've got to do something about Bob," he said. "He's not playing by the rules." I was told Bob allowed workers to come into the executive offices. Bob even fraternized with the workers, the sales manager told me with much consternation. "Some days Bob doesn't wear a tie. The next day the workers don't wear a tie, and Bob does. It's more than a problem; it's sheer anarchy." I was proud of myself when he said that because I didn't laugh.

Most employees, though, understood the symbolism Bob was putting across by running an open company. But it was quite difficult to explain to the sales manager the difference between freedom and anarchy.

There was another time, however, when the sales force's misinterpretation of our approach to business wasn't quite so funny. Once we had the factory up and running, we decided it was time to meet potential dealers in the United Kingdom to tell them about our company, our commitment to quality, and even more so, that it was nice to be their neighbors. We wanted them to understand us as people, not just as a faceless company. We viewed it as a sort of housewarming, although it wouldn't specifically be at our plant. We wanted to start things right, make a statement about ourselves.

The sales force we inherited said they would set the meeting up and take care of everything. "It will be a lovely time," they told us.

What we found, however, was that our own sales force really didn't have a clue about what we were trying to convey. Because of cultural differences or mere stubbornness on everyone's part, we had somehow failed to ingrain in the sales force the spirit of The North Face.

They set up the meeting in the Lake District, which is beautiful—pastoral and serene with rolling, picturesque hills. Streams and lakes dot the countryside, and trees abound. Driving to the meeting, I felt energized. The scenery was perfect for our image. But something went wrong. We turned away from the scenery into the grounds of the Clawthorpe Hotel. It was as if the sales manager had searched his entire life to find the one ugly spot in the midst of all that beauty.

I tried to stay positive as we walked inside. The display room had no lights and no heat. The dining room, I soon found out, operated for only two hours—serving cold sandwiches. The sales manager had arranged for no drinks. He thought it would save money. I knew it would cost plenty—plenty of sales. A cash bar was incredibly unfriendly. But I closed my eyes and took a deep breath. Stay in control, I told myself. It can't be that bad.

It was worse. The sales manager who had told me "Don't worry, I'll take care of everything" stood up and gave his speech. "Welcome," he said. "I wish I could stay here with you, but I promised the missus I'd take her to the symphony for her birthday. That is tonight. So I'll be leaving now and turning the meeting over to Hap. Enjoy yourselves."

I was flabbergasted. He had told me nothing of the symphony prior to that moment. I had no prepared speech. But I knew that my actions right then would make a statement about The North Face for years to come. I smiled and went on verbal automatic pilot.

I told Bob, "Find some solutions, quick. Arrange for free drinks, good food, and especially another place down the road where we can put across the image, as we know it, of The North Face—a friendly, caring company. We must salvage this."

I turned to the crowd of dealers and began to describe our company, our philosophy, and our mission. I interspersed adventuring stories with our business tenets while I waited for Bob to return. He came through, as I knew he would, and the meeting took a turn for the better.

For years afterward, whenever we met with our dealers, we managed to get a good laugh by just saying the word "Clawthorpe." At the time it wasn't funny at all, but it came to symbolize our mutual struggles.

In Scotland we managed to turn a bad experience into a humorous symbol of early difficulties. It would have been easy to be bitter about the whole thing. It could have come to symbolize many things if it had been handled differently. It certainly could have come to symbolize our ineptitude and lack of caring. But I had known better. I knew we were not inept. I knew we cared. What that meeting symbolized for me was just another learning experience on the long road of life.

I can laugh about it now because it *is* funny. Tragedies had better become comedies, or else you're in a lot of trouble. If a tragedy remains a tragedy forever, it's a symbol of a negative force running loose in your psyche.

It is important to be positive, to truly believe success is possible. Symbolism as a method of leadership is incredibly effective. But first you must convince yourself. If you've got the energy, the rest is easy.

7

TAPPING THE INFINITE UPSIDE:

Good Employees Know Their Jobs

Employees are your greatest asset—the one essential for any company. It's so simple, yet not many executives see it, or they ignore it if they do. Of all the business essentials, and there are hundreds, people are by far the most important. I'd rather have a company with great people and no money than the other way around. Money doesn't guarantee good people, but good people will get you money. Guaranteed.

You can't get or keep good people if you don't treat them as such. And even if you can get and keep them, you cannot maximize their potential unless you excite, involve, and nurture them.

Unfortunately the norm in business is conformity—a black, muddy river going nowhere. And even when conformity gets daring, it doesn't roar out individuality. It insults and demeans.

Let me give you an example: I was not the only one at The North Face who didn't fit in at Proctor & Gamble. Mike Ravizza, a vice president of retail, found himself to be a misfit as well.

Mike was out with his immediate supervisor one day following a typical salesman's day, calling on accounts.

It was 40 percent of the time driving, 40 percent sitting in the waiting room, and 20 percent selling. Mike's boss wasn't happy. Everywhere they went, they had to wait.

In the car between calls the supervisor lectured Mike about "respect." To Mike it seemed a strange word to use. But to his supervisor it was very important—like a title. He told Mike that Proctor & Gamble was the biggest and best in the industry. "We deserve respect," he said.

On the third call of the day the boss showed he was lost as to what the word "respect" means. There were eight people in the waiting room, sitting in stiff plastic chairs while they paged through old *Reader's Digest*s and pretended to enjoy such articles as "The Wonderful Things About Living Alone." They sat down, Mike and his boss. They sat for five minutes, and then the boss grabbed Mike's arm and said, "Come on outside. We've got to talk. I'm going to teach you the art of selling." They went outside and closed the door.

"You can't just sit there," said the boss. "You have to make yourself noticed." He talked to Mike as if he were teaching him to tie his shoes. "Tomorrow I want you to go into town to a kids' store and buy one of those Mickey Mouse hats. The ones with the ears, the cute little ears. Then I'll tell you what to do. Next time you're stuck in a waiting room, you pull out your mouse ears and put them on. Trust me. When the buyer comes out, he'll notice you. You'll stand out."

Mike said three words, "No *fucking* way." He turned and walked off. He walked 15 miles home, and the next day he walked into The North Face, where I hired him.

Demeaning employees is no way to excite them or motivate them. No one deserves to be treated as anything less than a thriving, pulsing human spirit with individual dreams, wants, and expectations. Dignity is a right.

You don't have to be as obvious as suggesting Mickey Mouse ears to insult an employee's dignity. It is just as easy to ignore their opinions. All too often employees, though experts on their particular realm, are ignored because their opinion conflicts with the preconceived notions of titled authority.

Robert Service ran into this. His parents were Baptist missionaries, and he was raised in Shanghai. Because of this and his raw intelligence he became an expert on China for the State Department. He had perspective. But he didn't have support—he worked for the State Department in the early 1950s. It was the McCarthy era, and Service recommended the United States support Mao Tse-tung because that was who the Chinese people supported. The U.S. government supported Chiang Kai-shek, an exploiter and known throughout China as such. It didn't matter; Mao was a communist, and the United States didn't like communists. Service also was labeled communist and fired.

He was undaunted. He landed a job with an East Coast electronics firm and rose to the presidency. Years later, when the company was sold for a large profit, he went on to the University of California for a Ph.D. in history. He was of an age when most people think about retirement, but he was back at school. It was fun for him in the classes on Chinese history—telling firsthand accounts to academic "experts" who had never visited the country. It was as if Service were teaching the course.

In the early 1970s the United States finally recognized it would need to deal with Mao if it wanted to deal with China. President Nixon assigned Henry Kissinger to figure a way to establish relations with the Chinese. Kissinger contacted Service, who was asked to do the preliminary groundwork. It was incredible irony, working for Nixon, one of the strong supporters of McCarthyism.

Lesser men would have quit when confronted with such obstacles—using former put-downs as justification for giving up or holding grudges forever. But Service is extraordinary, an enthusiastic battler who rolls with punches and then sets his sights on the next conquest. He has a saying that epitomizes his philosophy: "It's not the mountain that wears you down, it's the grain of sand in your shoes."

Bureaucracy is an obvious grain of sand. In America there was a heady period from World War II until the Vietnam War when business, though successful, became bloated, and bureaucracies increased the distance from the top of an organization to the bottom. Leaders lost touch with followers.

It has always amazed me that the Catholic Church has thrived for nearly 2,000 years with only six layers of management but General Motors needs 14 levels. Why GM needs 14 levels eludes me. It's a disease and a plague.

Bureaucracy. For years leaders have cut themselves off from their followers and relied on "organization" to provide motivation. American companies have become petrified.

Old-boy networks are rampant while new perspectives are shunned for fear of truth and enlightenment. It is a prejudiced system with the mechanisms of men's clubs and a heavy reliance on specific business and law schools.

Women were excluded from the executive levels of business. Fortunately that grave mistake is now being rectified.

Whoever was the prophet of this modern form of management should be hung over the doors of business in much the same way Genghis Khan hung cheating tax collectors over their own doors. We have been cheated out of a human form of leadership.

We have been denied common sense and offered instead an ineffective and inhuman science called "management." Business has become stratified and bureaucratized.

It doesn't have to be that way. With a human approach communication can flourish across the imaginary borders of title and authority. Some executives would contend that the problem is that employees don't think. I contend the problem is they are not allowed to think.

At The North Face we had two employees, John Kirschner and Bill Werlin, who were downhill ski fanatics, and they both wanted the company to expand into downhill ski clothing. I was dead set against it.

The problem, as I saw it, was that The North Face had established a reputation for making the very best truly functional equipment, and downhill skiers as a group cared more about fashion than function. I believed downhill ski equipment by its very nature was inconsistent with our company image—an image based on function more than anything else. Our equipment always did what it was supposed to. If it looked good, that was a bonus.

But Kirschner and Werlin weren't convinced. Every

time I turned them down, they'd come back with even more details on why I was wrong. Their views were based on the market and the reasoning of people like Theodore Levitt, the business theorist who suggested one reason railroads went out of business was because they didn't see the big picture. According to Levitt, railroad companies never saw themselves as being in the transportation business, but rather just in railroads.

"It's the same with us," said Kirschner and Werlin. "We can do more than just backpacking and mountaineering."

"No way," I said.

"Fine," they said. And a couple of weeks later they were back in my office again.

The most amazing thing is that these two were almost exact opposites. Werlin was flamboyant, sales and marketing oriented. Kirschner was into detail and precision. They were not the kind to be drawn to each other. Except, of course, for one thing—their mutual love of skiing.

They just attacked the project, and me—in a kind way, of course. They were determined. What they explained to me over and over was that there was a large market of skiers who needed equipment that worked. These skiers, said Werlin and Kirschner, had been abandoned by most of the industry, which had, as I knew, gone to fashion.

Finally their intensity and logic won me over. The way I figured it, these guys believed in the idea of expanding into downhill ski equipment so much that it was worth the risk to give it a try. They became our product champions. What we created was a ski clothing line based on something we called Extreme Gear. The name to the public meant it was for extreme conditions. Our inside joke was that it was extremely expensive.

But it sold. I was wrong. Werlin and Kirschner were

right, and the new ski line sold what we called tonnage—a hell of a lot. The uniforms were eventually chosen for instructors at over 100 ski areas including Aspen and Vail.

It would have been easy to remain stubborn in my refusal, basking in the false glory of a titled ego. Many executives do just that, certain they know more about everything than their underlings.

It's depressing to listen to most executives talk about business. They use the jargon they learned in business school—phrases such as "cost of capital" and "internal rates of return." They think they sound intelligent and logical, as if their removed, impersonal style has all the answers.

But they miss the point. It's clear when they speak to their employees. In the minds of many so-called leaders, success has nothing to do with people. They see all the profits, machinery, and plans as essential, but they view their work force as a burden. It's so sad.

The truth is people are the greatest asset of any company—the only one with an infinite upside. Machines and facilities wear down. They depreciate. And as time goes on, they become obsolete.

But a highly motivated, creative employee can return many times over what he or she costs. The key, of course, is not just to hire them but to listen to them and empower them. If you do, the rewards are tremendous.

Teresita Perez is tremendous. She was one of my employees, a smiling little dynamo from the Philippines—dedicated, intelligent, and highly skilled. Terry was one of the first people we hired, an original member of The North Face family. In the factory she was a sort of matriarch to the other workers.

She was always smiling. She worked in the finishing department of our factory, doing thread trimming and final quality inspection of our products. Hers was a busy job, and she was happy and proud of her work.

One day, a few years after we hired her, she came into my office crying. We had grown a lot—we had about 500 employees, so I didn't see her every day anymore. But here she was in my office crying. She was visibly shaken. I didn't know what to think. I was afraid something horrible had happened. Something had, she told me. The down-filled jackets her department was processing had defects, yet almost 100 had made it past three quality control inspectors and past her supervisor. She felt terrible. She didn't want to get anyone in trouble, but she knew The North Face's image of quality. The products weren't up to those standards, as she explained it. They could destroy the image of the company. It wasn't right, she said. It was tearing her up personally.

I supported her. There was nothing to that decision—if she cared so much and had been with the company so long, her judgment was fine by me. The jackets were brought back and, of course, she was right.

I don't think it's possible for any leader to feel more proud or touched than I did at that moment. I knew my vision of quality had connected to her. She knew my door was open and I wanted to hear from my employees. She knew more about her job than I did. All I had to do as a leader was recognize her expertise. My job was easy.

Leadership is creating an atmosphere of trust. You have to listen to employees, and then back up what you say. You have to treat people like people, not morons, and not like machines.

If all your employees are idiots, what does that say about you—the person who hired them? Listen and reward them. Recognize them. Every year at The North Face we'd recognize employees by giving them little trophies for years of service. You wouldn't believe how important those were. Recognition has to be given with class and humor and absolute sincerity. You have to be a leader, but first you must be a partner.

One Friday after work I went out with some of my executives and we began talking about what we saw as a discrepancy in our company: most of our management time and effort went toward our subpar employees, trying to get them up to our standards. We had unfairly overlooked our superior performers. They were really the ones who deserved our attentions. They deserved some recognition.

We came up with the Golden Trimmers Award. Trimmers are the pincerlike hand tools used in cutting threads from garments. Trimmers are constantly sharpened, but after extensive use they have to be replaced. We bronzed a few discarded trimmers. We decided to put them on a pegboard with a tribute to the winners I wrote up and our corporate seal. It wasn't expensive, and it didn't take a long time. But it did take caring. In a formal ceremony we acknowledged their contribution. Something like this could easily come across as an empty gesture, but it wasn't. It was genuine. Our great employees deserved recognition, and this was something from the heart—something uniquely The North Face.

Six years later I was invited to the home of one of our employees for a special dinner celebration. It was a major celebration—the attainment of her U.S. citizenship. All of the employee's immediate family was there, as were her cousins, nieces, nephews, uncles, and aunts. After I had been introduced to everyone, I happened to look on her mantel. There were photos of her children, a beautiful vase, and, yes, the Golden Trimmers Award. I knew then that what we had done six years earlier mattered. It had worked.

Rather than a huge, faceless bureaucracy that relies on rules and authority, it is always better to have some sort of informal network of human contact that lets employees know they are trusted.

One way we did this was by holding our long-range planning meetings far from the buildings of The North Face. We went to locations that allowed people to interact. Frequently we'd go to Trout Lake, 1,300 acres of unspoiled paradise near Spokane, Washington. It was my parents' place—it's very special to me.

The stated goal was to come up with a plan. The parallel goal was to have fun. It was a retreat, a gathering of minds—a chance to connect much deeper than was possible in the hectic world of business. We played games, we fished, we mountain biked, we had contests, and we gathered in groups. We talked, drank beer, and got to know one another better. It was work. Yeah, right. It was fun. Sure, we accomplished a lot. But what we accomplished even more than an agreement on our plan was a renewed enthusiasm—a rebirth of the collective spirit. We were rejuvenated.

We focused on people. We rejoiced at individuality—as long as it was focused on common goals. Everything was done with thoughts of family, opportunity, freedom. The goals were always quality, energy, creativity. Differences were more than tolerated; they were celebrated.

The North Face was the ultimate melting pot—at any one time we had 14 different languages spoken in our company, five used regularly in our written communication. We had employees from every part of the globe—Asia, Europe, South America, the United States, you name it.

One day the mayor of Berkeley brought a group of

visiting Soviets to see our factory. The Soviets were mostly impressed and asked incisive questions. But there was one who didn't fit in with the rest. At first I noticed his clothes—better tailored and higher-quality fabric. Soon I figured out he was the Communist party representative, since none of the others talked to him. When I told them about the variety of people who worked for us, most of the Soviets were impressed by the open culture in our company. But not the one who stood alone. He asked, "Is the real reason that you hire all these immigrants to exploit them for low wages?"

"No," I explained, "our employees are paid better by us than our competitors. The real reason we hire anyone is because we think they can produce quality. Quality is not something that has geographic barriers or definitions."

The idea in all personnel decisions is to foster community—eliminate the toxic envy that plagues many companies. The way to do this is to let people be themselves.

Employees look to leaders for how a job should be done. They will emulate or approximate that style as long as they can do it within the boundaries of their own personality. It's a fine line to walk, but it's easy if you know how. Employees want guidelines and vision, but then they want to be left alone to flourish as they see fit. They want constant access to you, but they don't want you leaning over their shoulder. They really want you out of the way so they can take over and perform. They want vision, control, and creativity.

W. L. Gore is a company that offers all of this. Gore makes a number of products, but the best known is a waterproof, breathable fabric, Gore-tex. It revolutionized the outdoor apparel market. The company was founded by William Gore, who had previously worked for E. I. du Pont. It was at Du Pont that Gore began to think about a new way of motivating people. When he founded his own company, he put it into effect. He called it the lattice work system.

At Gore everyone is described as an "associate" and treated as an equal. They use the analogy of a boat on the water to explain what level of decisions can be risked by employees. They described decision making as drilling holes in the side of the boat. Any holes drilled below the waterline must be reviewed by others. In other words, risk is good, but don't risk everything. If a decision is large enough to affect the health of the whole organization, then the whole organization should be brought into the decision-making process. But small mistakes won't significantly wound the company, and the reward of small mistakes is that the employees will learn. And Gore, using this philosophy, has become phenomenally successful.

Every time employees learn, they improve. To constantly leave decisions in the hands of superiors kills motivation and may cost you expertise. After all, someone doing a job eight hours a day usually knows more about that particular activity than his or her boss. Authority does not equal knowledge.

A few years ago I decided I would try the sport of ultralight airplane flying, and I saw firsthand why one should not blindly trust anyone putting himself off as an authority.

Flying these tiny planes looked like fun, and it required no pilot's license. It offered a chance to get into the backcountry quickly, and I could land the plane virtually anywhere.

The salesman was all hype, a vision in polyester—he liked me from the instant he saw me, or so he said. "It's simple," he explained. "These are the safest planes around because they are incredibly sturdy and their light weight makes the glide ratio so good." I was skeptical. The plane looked flimsy—just a skeleton and a propeller.

But still, it did look like a hell of a lot of fun. I like fun. He explained to me I could master flying the plane in one day, and without a license I could be flying solo the next day.

I grilled him a bit. I asked how difficult the planes were to maintain. "I'm not very mechanically inclined," I said. "How can I be sure everything is as it ought to be?"

"Don't worry," he said. "I know all about these planes. Everything's perfect. I've only been flying these a short time myself. But they're so easy, I learned it all in one day, just like you will."

I was ready to go for it. What the hell—life is short, have dessert first and all of that.

He collected my money, and we began to push the ultralight to the takeoff area. Another man came and helped. The second man's hands were greasy—I presumed he was a mechanic. As we were pushing, the mechanic made small talk. But then, after pushing a short way, he stopped and turned to the salesman. From easy conversation, his face had become serious. "Where is the wing nut?" asked the mechanic. "The one that bolts the right wing down?"

The salesman responded, "What wing nut? I've never seen one on that bolt and I've been flying this thing for weeks."

"The wing can be wrenched off without it," said the mechanic. He fished a wing nut from his pocket and installed it. "You're damn lucky."

I was flabbergasted. But the mechanic assured me everything was fine now, so I decided to try it.

The flight was exhilarating. But I was wary—what else was there about the plane that the salesman didn't know? I never did buy the plane, though admittedly it was lots of fun. I wasn't going to have a mechanic around, and I knew what I didn't know. The salesman obviously didn't. I wasn't an expert on the planes, and neither was my supposed teacher. His authority proved false.

If you want the truth, go for knowledge, not authority. And if you want your employees to have knowledge, you have to reward it with trust and honesty—a willingness to involve them in decisions that affect their own job. Employees must be allowed to grow. They have to be excited and motivated.

Al Hildebrand understands this. He is a large man, a onetime draft pick of the Houston Oilers. He never made the team, but he used his football bonus money to pay his way through business school. He had a successful 25-year career with Spectra-Physics, a San Francisco Bay area company specializing in laser beams.

He retired at 49, well off and happy. At a business school reunion on the day he retired, I asked him what satisfied him most about his career at the company. It wasn't the wealth, he said. It wasn't the title of vice president.

Rather, it was two things. The first was that he put his physics training to good use by inventing six items that received patents. The second gave him even more satisfaction, he said. "I led, managed, and encouraged eleven subordinates who later became CEOs of Silicon Valley companies." He was most proud, he said, that the people under him flourished.

When leaders recognize that individual growth leads to organizational growth, they have found the key to the kingdom. A company such as Spectra-Physics that loses 11 employees to their own dreams is much stronger than a company that never loses anyone to personal ambition. It is essential to feed and nurture personal ambition. Sure, you'll lose a few people to their own dreams. But is it really a loss? When a child grows up, do you lose that child?

Of course not. As Hildebrand said, nothing gave him more pride. The two most important things to offer any child, any employee, are roots and wings. Roots to grow, and wings to fly. With both, potential is virtually limitless.

8

Wrestling with Gorillas:

Obstacles to Fulfilling Your Passion

There were these two guys, the Whittakers. Lou and Jim. Big guys, each six foot five. They were twins with lumberjack arms and the suntanned-sunburned look of perpetual outdoorsmen. Jim was the first American ever to scale Mt. Everest.

They were climbing on a windswept glacier with an expedition in Alaska. It was in the middle of nowhere, a desolate ice field; the winds howled. A member of the team got injured. He desperately needed medical attention. As the sun quickly began to slide over the horizon the temperature fell precipitously. The Whittakers knew they had to do something, and do it fast.

They called by radio for a helicopter to evacuate the injured person. Usually they would call in a jet helicopter to whisk an injured climber to safety, but there wasn't one available. They couldn't wait for one to become available—the man's condition was worsening. So they sent for a standard helicopter, one not well suited for high altitudes. It wasn't pretty. The landing was rough. But the helicopter did get there. They had to quickly load the climber into the helicopter because taking off in the dark would be impossible. They loaded him but had no time for relief. When the helicopter tried to lift back off the glacier, it couldn't. The air was too thin. The wind was blowing long, cold blasts, and the blades of the helicopter kicked out clouds of snow. With the light rapidly disappearing, the Whittakers knew it could be a matter of life and death for their companion. Pulmonary edema was just one of the fears.

Time was running out, so the Whittakers improvised. They each grabbed a rail of the helicopter and heaved it off the edge of the glacial cliff. The Whittakers watched—entranced by the object of their actions. Down it went, like a rock through the thin air. Finally, halfway down the blades of the helicopter caught air and it took off toward the hospital. Talk about audacity, talk about confidence—they had them both.

When Lou Whittaker told me that story, we were standing with a group of five people in the Las Vegas Hilton, the setting of the annual ski show. It was March, a few years ago.

Lou is a natural storyteller, a mountain man as comfortable in Las Vegas as he is in all the story-making places he's conquered. Lou loves the wild, even the wild of Las Vegas. He loves to laugh, and he loves to tell a story.

His voice got louder at the beginning. In the middle of the story it dropped down, and then it rose to a crescendo as the helicopter caught air. And unlike a lot of tall people, he didn't stoop to talk to me. He stood firm and erect, a bottle of beer in his hand and a wry smile on his face. "Whatever it takes," he concluded with a grin and a booming laugh.

Afterward I asked him, "But what if it hadn't worked?"

"Sometimes," mused Lou, "you just know."

Obstacles will inevitably pop up on the path to fulfilling your passion, and when they do you must, like the Whittakers did, listen to your instinct, your intuition, that little voice deep inside that "just knows."

Like all adventures, the adventure of leadership takes faith. Faith in yourself, and faith in anything and anyone that helps you maintain that faith.

In the adventure of business, as in life, most problems revolve around people, and their solutions demand your heart as much as your head.

At L. L. Bean, Leon Gorman, company president and the grandson of L. L. Bean, sits in on every product meeting. Gorman has the final say on what is included in the catalog. Much of it depends on market studies and sales records—all compiled professionally. But the final word on what goes in is Gorman's, and more than once he has ordered an item in, or out, of the book just because he felt it should be that way. He goes with his gut even when the so-called professionals tell him it's wrong, because he trusts an instinct that sits at the core of the L. L. Bean vision.

Have you ever been in a corporate boardroom? Most look like carefully crafted works of art, with carved mahogany swirling and angling this way and that—all of it a red-brown ode to power. But look closer, beyond the trappings of wealth, and see if you can find any good reason for such ostentatiousness. Then ask yourself, Where is the product? If it's not there, the company is in trouble.

If company leaders don't take the time to look at their organization's product, to feel it, to smell it, to taste it if necessary, then those leaders are merely along for the ride. They are enjoying the fruits without sharing the labor. They do not deserve respect, and they do not deserve to be called leaders. Most likely, they lack the feel, the intuition, and the passion necessary to make the right decisions on corporate matters. To be a leader you can't be a dilettante. You have to immerse yourself and get your hands dirty. It takes incredible determination.

In Berkeley, California, a company created the Power Bar, a candy-bar-type product specially formulated for athletes to eat before competition. It gave them energy. Standard chocolate bars did the same thing, but the chocolate in those bars could upset the athletes' stomachs—a disaster in competition.

The problem was manufacturing without chocolate. The solution was complicated because the machines that made traditional candy bars are lubricated by the chocolate in the bars. If you take the chocolate out, you take away the lubrication.

The people at Power Bar had to invent their own machinery—machinery some experts said couldn't be invented—that operated without the natural lubricant of chocolate. They wanted to produce a totally digestible, quick natural energy source. They succeeded on all counts.

It got to the point where U.S. cycling team members—led by people such as Davis Phinney of the 1988 Olympics—

demanded Power Bars. The Olympic committee said no. Power Bar was not an official supplier.

The cyclers nearly revolted, proclaiming they'd get Power Bars somehow. Within days the Olympic committee made Power Bar an official supplier, waving the requirement for sponsorship money. It was because the product was so good.

The people at Power Bar knew they were right, that they were making a substitute candy bar that was great for athletes—it was digestible and it enhanced their performance. And now they had proof that the market accepted their product, since Olympic cyclers were demanding it.

The people at Power Bar overcame two problems: the need for new machinery and an Olympic committee that was more wedded to the concept of raising sponsorship money than to the cyclists' nutrition. Instinctively Power Bar knew they could build the new machinery, but convincing the Olympic committee took more than instinct. It took dogged perseverance.

Imagine this scenario. You are Power Bar within your company. Your boss is the Olympic committee. You have invented a way to increase quality and efficiency in the company. But your boss says no. No way can that work; it's not in the company manual, says the Boss.

What should you say?

Here's what the people at Power Bar said: Rewrite the damn manual. Let's do whatever has to be done.

The determination to do whatever is required must, inevitably, be coupled with perseverance and irrepressible optimism to prevail.

H. Ross Perot, the head of EDS, had those attributes when two of his employees were taken hostage in Iran in 1979. He organized his executives into a commando team and went to Iran to break his people free. He even visited the jail himself, under an assumed name, to give the hostages confidence. Perot and his team broke them out of the jail and ran them across the Iranian border. That's passion. That's commitment. That's an instinct for knowing what needs to be done, and it's the guts to do it.

It takes more than just knowing what's right. It takes the fortitude to stand by your passion in the face of overwhelming obstacles.

The greatest commencement speech ever given was by Winston Churchill after World War II. It was an overcast day at his prep school alma mater, Harrow—one of many places he never excelled at academically.

Churchill walked up to the podium. He looked at the crowd, all decked out in their caps and gowns. Every eye was on him. And he said, "Never give up."

He looked again at the crowd. It stirred slightly at his pause. "Never *ever* give up," he said. He paused again. And finally he said, "Never give up." With that thought he turned from the podium and sat back down.

It is so simple yet so damned difficult, this idea of no surrender. It comes down to the essence of existence—a high-noon showdown with yourself. Do you have what it takes?

Or don't you?

How much do you believe in your instinct? It's easy to say, I know I'm right. It's another thing to go ahead and prove it. I believe in trying to prove my beliefs—the way I see it, the meek will inherit nothing.

George Lowe is a climber who failed in two attempts to climb the east face of Mt. Everest before he finally succeeded. The east face is tremendously challenging. If you've ever seen pictures, it looks basically like a vertical rope climb at 8,000 meters. Though there certainly is nothing easy about any side of Mt. Everest, the east face is unbelievable—it's a real "gorilla."

Just to attempt climbing the east face of Mt. Everest is heroic. But to go again, after twice failing—that takes absolute passion, determination, and perseverance.

When Lowe finally reached the top of Everest, he made a decision that was a bit selfish, yet in the realm of mountaineering completely understandable. He hacked off his support ropes after he came back down. He wanted others to take on the "gorilla" of the east face on their own just as he did. He was conquered by the passion of his sport, which was not bagging peaks but just plain mountaineering, with all its factors woven into one fabric—the planning, the pain, the struggle, and all of the luck associated with it.

What I am saying is that to persevere like a Power Bars or a Churchill or a George Lowe you must live life at its core, walking on the raw nerve where you can feel the golden terrain of existence—a gestalt on this breathing planet. You have to take it all in and learn and grow and come up with something to say at the end, just in case you get asked, "Do you have any regrets?"

My friend Nick Nichols bills himself as the Indiana Jones of photography. He sometimes works with Bernie Krause, who collects sounds all over the world. Bernie, in fact, has produced very successful compact disks using only the sounds of nature. They're incredible.

They went to Africa a short while after Diane Fossey died and did some advance work for the movie *Gorillas in the Mist*, and for Nick's books on gorillas. They lived one month over there. At first the primates thought Nick and Bernie were threatening them. At one point the gorillas picked the two of them up and started throwing them in the air.

In business you may not get thrown around by gorillas. But it can seem that way. The point is, you have to stick it out. You have to tough it out, you have to make the sacrifices.

Nichols and Krause did. By the end they fit in with the gorillas. They stayed there and kept acting as part of the environment, and actually they were.

They did what they wanted to do—they lived the fullest way they knew. Even though it meant getting thrown around, it was fun.

The gorillas of business can be just as hostile as those in the jungle. Your employees can be gorillas, your banker loves to be one, your competitors are by nature hostile gorillas, and even your customers will toss you around the minute something goes wrong. Every call a salesperson makes is to a gorilla. Some are nice, but think of this: The average number of calls a salesperson must make on a new account before closing a sale is five. The gorilla wins on the first four. The good salesperson keeps going back until eventually he, like Nichols and Krause, befriends the gorilla.

There was a businessman like this, named Karsten Solheim. Karsten invented a great set of golf clubs, but he had to take on two gorillas: no money to speak of to produce them, and no testing equipment to prove his product. He didn't let this deter him. Rather, he and his son hopped in his car and went into the desert. They blasted along at up to 100 miles per hour so Karsten's son could hold different clubs out the window to see which ones caused what aerodynamic resistance. The desert wasn't exactly the atmosphere of a test lab, but it didn't matter. Karsten and the company he founded, Ping, went on to do quite well.

Passion requires an uncommon nerve to face failure, disaster, shortages, and exhaustion and to stand back up and declare, Let's do it again. It takes absolute dedication to the task at hand. It is not a two-minute drill of instant ego gratification, but rather a continuous surge of energy into the gland that controls creativity and internal drive. Passion is a fluid vision of the future.

Ned Gillette is an explosion of vision—like an astronaut, a cowboy, and an engineer rolled into one human form. Gillette, with dark shaggy hair and wire-rim glasses, is thin, almost skinny, and in his 40s. His appearance is deceptive, though, because Gillette has phenomenal strength of both body and spirit.

In 1983 Ned approached me with his plan for a rowboat trip to Antarctica—one of the few "firsts" left in the adventuring world. It sounded crazy, but as I knew from my past dealings with him, Ned doesn't do crazy things. Oh sure, the vision started with a crazy idea. "It usually does," said Ned. Rowing to Antarctica certainly stretched the traditional bounds of sanity.

But Ned has a multidimensional view of his adventures, and the very first dimension he explores is that of safety. Ned's is never a half-cocked light bulb of inspiration that fades into the memory of late-night braggadocio. His was a precise, step-by-step consideration of a problem—rowing through the Drake Passage, called by many the roughest seas in the world—and subsequent development of a solution.

What appeared to the outside world to be the sexiest hell-on-wheels adventure in the history of mankind was really a small-scale NASA-type project with every contingency covered. Ned spent four years planning the trip, getting sponsors—including The North Face—and studying the weather patterns of the 600-mile stretch of open ocean that has been known to launch up to 60-foot seas and smash clipper ships like toothpicks.

What makes Ned brilliant is that he is the perfect left brain–right brain mix. He has an almost Zen intuition about what will work and a persevering gut that won't allow failure. He also has a work ethic and a dedication to detail that manufacture the vision of passion. A former member of the U.S. Olympic ski team and a dropout from an MBA program, Gillette tried a stint at selling encyclopedias before he happened on his career as a professional adventurer. What he did was become the best in the world.

For years Ned planned and worked. It was staggering—designing the boat, raising the money for the expedition, learning the unique weather patterns of Drake Passage. There was so much more. This was no mere project; it was a voluntary trek through the wild currents of a clipper ship cemetery—through waters that never rose above 31 degrees Farenheit. For four years he trained for what eventually became a 21-day sojourn into water that Sir Francis Drake in 1578 described as *"the most mad seas."*

Finally he and three crew members went to Chile, to Cape Horn at the southern tip of South America. And they waited. What they were waiting for was a window of opportunity. First the ice in the passage had to melt. Then they needed to wait for the right day, with the right wind, to launch out into those mad seas. The right wind, if it comes at all, comes only during one month a year, and even then it is quite unpredictable. They knew that once they set off for Antarctica, they wouldn't be able to come back. If they stopped before Antarctica, the current would overpower and sweep them off toward the south of Africa—a journey of weeks or months that no one on their vessel might survive.

The ice never melted that year. Ned had to scrap his plan and wait for an entire year. During that year one of Ned's partners took $35,000 of the money Ned had raised to finance the trip and spent it on himself. Rather than get discouraged by all the bad news, Gillette kept his promise to himself and pushed on the following year, when he and three others successfully rowed his bright-red ellipse of a boat—fondly named the Sea Tomato—to Antarctica.

He persevered. And when he completed the trip, as is always the case with Ned, he immediately displayed his professionalism and business acumen by keeping all the promises he'd made to all of his sponsors as well. Keeping promises is absolutely essential. Your reputation is only as good as your word.

Rather than waste time and let the experience become cold in his head, Ned immediately wrote down his thoughts. He wanted to make his presentations about the trip top notch. Also, he flew to Las Vegas for the annual backpacking and mountaineering show to speak to customers and employees of sponsoring companies. Needless to say, the sponsors, whom Gillette fondly thanked during his many public presentations, were quite impressed. Ned is truly a *professional* adventurer.

And he is an ingenious professional. He found his passion, and he gutted out his adventure. He persevered. And every time one adventure ends for him, he ingeniously finds a way for someone to pay for him to go on another.

Ned has been faced with a problem of his own choosing—he wants to do things that have never been done before. This makes ingenuity essential. It's the same in business—business doesn't need historians; it needs visionaries. The world is changing too fast to rely on old solutions.

Ingenious decision making in an organization can ignite

a spark of excitement that redundant decision making doesn't. Ingenuity inspires. In business you have to be a Ned Gillette. You have to do what hasn't been done before. You have to live your adventure to the fullest and constantly strive for better solutions.

Another adventurer is Cliff Crilly, who learned the hard way why it was important for him to outlast a sensory-deprivation tank before he was allowed to go to Antarctica. Unlike Gillette, who wanted to experience going to Antarctica, Crilly wanted to experience *living* in Antarctica.

The sensory-deprivation tank was hard enough. It was completely dark, and the tank was filled with a thick, warm liquid that created no waves. The first time Crilly went in, he stayed there for what seemed to be hours. When he finally came out, he was told he'd been inside for one entire minute. Sixty seconds.

The next time he went in, he counted his heartbeat. He thought he had been inside for quite some time. But when he came out, they said he had stayed inside for only four minutes—which says something about the speed of his heartbeat.

Again Crilly went into the sensory-deprivation tank. But that time the operators of the tank had to tap on Crilly's shoulder 3½ hours later. He had found peace inside the tank. He was happy.

Onward to Antarctica went Crilly, who is, by the way, a good friend. He was on a mapping expedition with one other explorer in a mountainous region near the South Pole. Suddenly it was as if a wall of weather came at them, and they were overcome by a whiteout. An absolute whiteout that took visibility to zero. It made walking impossible. Vertigo was their daily partner. They could do nothing but wait out the storm.

They set up camp and went to sleep. When they awoke, it was the same—blowing snow; swirling, gusting, blindness. They were stuck.

But they had a small radio, and so they called out for food drops from rescue airplanes. They found the food by walking in concentric circles around their tent while tethered to it so they wouldn't get lost.

Days passed. The weather stayed the same. It got worse, if anything. It all became a strange routine. Word games and card games and stories and endless hours of self-examination. At some point, I don't care what Crilly says, he must have thought: What the hell am I doing here?

Thirty-one days passed. Thirty-one. All along, Crilly knew the answer to his question. He was waiting for the weather to pass so he could get on with his mapping expedition.

Look at the faces of people when you walk through life. Many have a set, comfortable, dull glare. No animation, no drive, and no vitality. Very few have the eyes of a Cliff Crilly, willing to endure almost anything to achieve his goal. Instead the look is one of settled acceptance—of someone beaten down by fraudulent authority for so long that there is no energy to fight on. It's sad, so much wasted human potential.

It doesn't have to be that way. We as leaders can save America from this drudgery. What it will take is an infusion of passion—the pulsing grip of any great vision. We must give up the security of tradition for the surprise of passion. We are all driven by inner needs, and not just the survivalistic ones either. We are driven by a need to accomplish, to express ourselves, to succeed, and to contribute to society. Everyone, I don't care who, wants to do something great with his or her life. Many never even acknowledge that want. It becomes hidden, a source of shame.

But desire for greatness is not shameful. It is something to be celebrated—something to be nurtured. People in business, just like Crilly, are willing to endure great hardship if it will bring the fruits of life—success, recognition, and the heartbeat-by-heartbeat thrill of existence that comes from accomplishment.

Dreams are wonderful. But dreams alone, as Walter Mitty showed us, are not enough. When nothing surfaces alongside the dream—when there is no passion—there is only the passing thought. There must be a real life boring in—an entrenchment of the soul, if you will, in the logistics of the dream to make it come true. It takes the dedication of Ned Gillette with the perseverence of Churchill. And it takes the ingenuity of both.

Many aspiring leaders believe they must be dispassionate, but I'll be damned if I know why. Passion is magnetic, it draws people to you, but some managers are so dispassionate they won't even own a dog. One way to express passion is to cry, really cry, when you lose a sale, and rejoice when you close one. You have to care. Despite uncertainty, you have to let your heart lead you. It will usually be right, and it will certainly draw your co-workers in around you. Allowing passion into your life not only empowers you as a leader, it also allows you to have fun. Don't just excite, incite.

The level of dedication of a superb leader is almost infinite. If you have it, you exude passion. As a leader you must ask others to dig deep. The only way that will sell is if you, the leader, dig deeper. You have to show a willingness to sacrifice, a capacity for the audacious, and an instinct for brilliance.

A leader cannot be detached or robotic. A leader must

be involved, putting emotions up front where everyone can see that the task at hand is more than just a way to make money. A leader must inspire, but first a leader must be inspired.

Phil Knight, the founder of Nike, was inspired. Back when Nike was a small company in Oregon, Knight knew he had a great product. But he couldn't get anyone to finance his concept without stealing the company from him. He wanted to grow, and he knew a huge market existed for his athletic shoes if he could find the money—enough to feed explosive growth. He didn't just believe, he *knew* there was a market for his shoes.

Knight went to Nisho Iwaii, the Japanese trading company that had supplied him with some components. I believe it was laces and soles, but some people say it was even less than that.

Knight said, "I've got this great idea. There's only one little thing you've got to do for me—you've got to lend me the money so I can manufacture more shoes. Not only will you receive interest on the money you lend me, but also I could buy more from you. You could double or triple the interest with the profit you'd make on the things you sell me."

Nisho Iwaii understood the risk but saw the opportunity. They went forward and helped Knight create the new-booming sneaker industry. Knight paid off the trading company as soon as he had sold his shoes to retailers. But up to that point Nisho Iwaii financed Nike, helping Knight grow. As Knight proved, you can be pretty creative under pressure.

Like Knight, I had the usual difficulty getting financing when I first came up with my plan for The North Face. Everyone I went to turned me down. It was one of the most frustrating periods of my life. I just knew I was right. Finally, when the last venture capital (by then I had renamed them all "vulture capital") firm I talked with turned me down, I looked them right in the eye and said, "Fine. I understand your rejection, but do me a favor. Make me a bet. I'll bet you $500 that in five years The North Face will be worth more than two-thirds of the companies in your portfolio are." They never did bet me. They were, however, so intrigued that they reconsidered and financed The North Face. Five years later I would've easily won the bet.

It was easy for me to be passionate and persevere, because my spark was a personal one. Always I strove for more.

Although The North Face was founded on the principle of making the best-possible products, in 1970 I decided we needed to do even better—to improve the best. I didn't want to just dominate the market, I wanted to revolutionize it. Through a friend I contacted Buckminster Fuller, the inventor of the geodesic dome. My idea was to get Bucky to help design a geodesic-dome tent. It didn't exactly work out that way, but it did work out.

Bucky wrote back full of enthusiasm. He was convinced he knew exactly what we needed but, unfortunately, was without time for the project. So without Bucky's design, I waited. I waited more than five years. While I waited, I began bouncing the idea off some of my employees. I wanted, needed really, to find some people who shared my belief that a geodesic-dome tent was possible and would make all the tents on the market obsolete. I needed people who understood my premise—to evangelize this cause within the company. I found two people with just that vision.

The first was Bruce Hamilton, a dope-smoking hippie, graduate of the University of Vanderbilt, and disciple of

Karl Marx. He was not your typical corporate employee by any stretch. At times, when Karl Marx was particularly fresh in Bruce's mind, we'd go around and around about the strengths and weaknesses of capitalism and communism. These were not mere discussions of theory, either. Often Bruce had a problem with the capitalistic way I ran The North Face. Through it all, though, we became friends.

Bruce had a math degree and was somewhat of a Buckminster Fuller groupie. He, honest to God, spent a year on the road like a devoted Deadhead (as in The Grateful Dead), following Fuller from city to city to hear him speak.

When I went to Bruce with my ideas for a geodesic-dome tent, he was more than enthralled. He was ecstatic. It was like asking a Deadhead to tune Jerry Garcia's guitar.

The second person was Mark Erickson, also an iconoclast—part hippie, part artist—who was dedicated to doing something special with his life. He was a graduate of Northwestern. In Berkeley the counter-culture types seemed to flock to us. We had established a reputation of being open to all types. Not only did we welcome them, but for many we were a last-ditch chance at a life of steady employment. At The North Face we loved this image.

Mark applied for a job with The North Face 28 times. Yes, that's right. No misprint—28 times. He saw himself as the epitome of a North Face employee. Finally we did too.

He took the only job we had—as a janitor. Of course, in our company this didn't limit him. We encouraged people to rise above their daily duties and do anything possible to help the company be the best. Mark responded. Boy, did he.

Mark was in love with design and creation, and he immediately identified with the project. Employees naturally self-selected into projects that interested them, and this was a project he relished. Mark, who had long since risen from janitor into product design, was perfect for the geodesic-dome tent—he had an analytical mind, a creative disposition, and the flexibility necessary for the creative process. Hiring Mark was half luck and half brilliance—our luck, his brilliance. Whatever, he quickly rose in the company by displaying a great visual sense—the geodesic tent is a tribute to his aesthetic skills. Mark now owns a design firm.

Mark and Bruce set out to design the tent that would revolutionize the world market for backpackable tents. Soon Bucky came along to offer his input. Mark and Bruce were in heaven. So was I. We combined Mark's product design with Bruce's mathematics, and into the mix jumped the legendary Buckminster Fuller, a hero to both Mark and Bruce. I knew the geodesic-dome tent would become what it became—the inspirational parent to at least the next ten generations of small backpackable tents.

Mark and Bruce collected what can only be called a cult of followers, wedded to the project and to the belief in the vision of geodesics as articulated by Buckminster Fuller. One of these followers, Jim Shirley, eventually went on to work on the world's weather and greenhouse-effect problems. This work was a direct result of the inspiration he received from working with Bucky. It was truly a magical time.

Nevertheless, there were plenty of difficulties along the way. For one thing, the tent poles that went through the bends of the tent were experiencing stress-corrosion cracking—a technical way of saying they were breaking. At one point we recalled every pole we ever put in our product. Making good on our warranty was our normal way of doing business.

I'll never forget the day we finally unveiled the original tent, designed just for Bucky. It was October 7, 1977, our son's ninth birthday. Bucky spoke at the ceremony, and then we had a well-practiced team assemble an oversized version of our geodesic-dome tent in ten minutes. Everyone who participated was a part of the team.

Following the ceremony, a few of us—Bucky included—headed over to my house. Bucky immediately took to my grandmother, who was two years older than he. They started talking about time, their lives—the first car, the first airplane, and so on. The rest of us just sat back and listened. It was one of the most educational evenings of my life. Finally, before the evening was over, Bucky walked up to my son, Matt, put his arm around Matt's shoulder, and wished him a happy birthday. And then he gave Matt a book he had authored. In it Buckminster Fuller wrote: "To Matt, on his ninth birthday—a member of the generation who is going to change mankind for the benefit of all humanity." Reading that later, I thought, We're all part of *that* generation.

Buckminster Fuller was a utopian. He and those of us at The North Face were not just trying to design a new tent—we wanted to improve the world. The tent was the focal point, but we were also thinking about an eventual market of people using tents as permanent residences instead of houses. We thought of it as good capitalism. With good capitalism we could change the world—allow people to explore the wilderness, appreciate nature, and stop the destruction of the planet.

We had created our dream and battled it out. When something didn't work at first, we figured out a way to make it work. We believed in it. We had taken our first step. It was time to start planning our next. Financially we created a monumentally successful project. Yet no one thought only in terms of making money.

We thought that by striving for our best—financially, physically, and spiritually—we would *be* our best. That tent was no mere product of fabric and metal—it was a physical representation of our lives for the past five years. Every hiker who purchased that tent was, in effect, joining us on our incredible journey. We weren't just selling hikers tents. We were selling them five very special years of our lives. We were selling them our best friend, our pet gorilla.

9

IMPROVING PERFECTION:

Only the Best Will Do

Chicago. There was a wrath of January wind and a swirling, throbbing snowfall that moved like a bad headache. It was so cold my face burned. The sky was gone—in its place, a gray, infinite void. No moon, no stars; only cold.

I had just left a sporting-goods show at McCormick Place on the frozen banks of Lake Michigan. I was with my vice president of retail, Tom Applegate. As soon as we walked outside we expected to flag down a taxi, but no such luck. What we flagged down was less a taxi than a mobile dumpster. It was grimy, with oil stains everywhere, and the floor was a puddle. But it was five below zero and we had already waited a half hour. It would have to do. The cab driver had the semi-crazed look endemic to big-city cab drivers, along with a two-day growth of beard and a shock of unruly hair.

When we got in, there was a problem. One of the back doors was broken and wouldn't stay shut. When we pointed this out to the driver, he told us he couldn't take us because the broken door was too dangerous. But we wouldn't leave. We had been outside so long that even my hair was cold.

Tom and I examined the door and quickly figured that the rocker arm on the door latch was the problem and could be easily repaired by hand. However, it was covered with grease and grime. It didn't make sense to work on it in our business clothes—we had another meeting to attend. The cabbie looked at us, confused. He wasn't sure he understood our explanation. To test it he went to the other door and pushed down hard on the latch on that door, replicating the malfunction of the first door. Then he stopped, dumbfounded.

With that push, the problem doubled—we now had two broken doors. I was anxious. I was cold. I had a meeting to attend, but the cabbie was now more insistent than ever that he couldn't take us. My retort was that if he had to get back to the shop for repairs, he couldn't get there without us. We could help.

And we did. Sitting in the backseat, Tom and I each grabbed opposing door handles with our hands and linked our other arms together—structurally linking one side of the cab to the other. This kept the doors from flying open and us from falling out. Using this improvised latching technique, we helped the cabbie get to the shop. When we got there, we finally flagged a "real" cab to take us on to our meeting.

It's a simple thing, to expect a cab to have doors that close and a decor that doesn't come from the junkyard. But so often we find that even our least expectations cannot be met. The problem is that so few people pay attention to quality. In an economic climate where quick money rules, quality has become a joke. But the joke's on us.

Almost every company has some sort of quality control program. Unfortunately most are just statistical tools designed to weed out defects, and not even all of them. Quality control programs don't add to quality; they merely attempt to keep it from dropping to the unacceptably low level that no one will buy. That's the problem—an American infatuation with meeting the lowest common denominator and the knee-jerk acceptance of the unfounded axiom that the consumer will always take price over performance.

I remember reading an interview with one of the astronauts upon his return from a successful space mission. He was asked what he was thinking as he sat in the capsule ready to blast off. "I was thinking," he said, "that all the parts of the spaceship went to the lowest bidder."

That says it all. The lowest bidder! Not the best; the lowest. The cheapest. Sure, he got home all right. But still—the lowest bidder. It's become the American way to worry about price first and quality second.

This is not to say that quality always has to be the most expensive. Often it is; many times it isn't. Quality isn't about money, it's about caring. It's about wanting to be the best because there is personal pride at stake—an individual declaration of identity with the product.

There is always a market for the best, all over the globe. It's an obvious and well-known fact that mountain climbers don't like to buy discounted climbing ropes. And there's the joke about the parachute offer for sale—cheap, slightly irregular, but used only once. When something is as important as life and death—and all business decisions should be—quality is irreplaceable.

For everyone involved, it's a lot more fun to pursue the top of the market than any other segment. It's more challenging—it's energizing.

Making the best ensures that a company gets repeat customers while offering an umbrella of protection against excessive competition. Quite simply, few companies are willing to compete at the top end of the market.

Great quality can differentiate you from all the others in your field. There is an aura about quality—a glow you feel when you are involved in the event of quality. There is a common bond of satisfaction shared by those involved with quality—a mutual energy perpetuated by being the best. Quality is not just a statement about products; it is the credo of a life style.

In the United States there are 500,000 brand names registered and actively used. Every consumer sees more than 875,000 advertising impressions each year. According to one retail study, there are enough stores in the United States to serve 500 million people—more than twice the 240 million population. These staggering numbers show how difficult it is to stand out. Yet to be successful, you must stand out. The best way, quite simply, is with the highest quality.

Quality will show up in the most unlikely places. Quality always stands out. Peter Glen, the critic and author, had a quality experience at, of all places, a coffee shop—in a Tokyo department store.

The first thing he noticed was the impeccably groomed staff waiting to serve him. Why? he asked. Why would a mere coffee shop in a department store have such well-groomed help?

The answer was pride, he was told. Pride of the manager, who personally inspected every employee and sent them home if they did not look immaculate. And pride of the employees. The manager went on to explain that all employees were required to speak two languages.

Imagine such a requirement in the United States, where many employees can't handle even one language. Americans would tell you it's superfluous; Japanese would tell you it's good business.

After talking with the manager, Peter ordered coffee. He was quickly given a hot towel to freshen himself, and it was promptly followed by his coffee—no ordinary cup of coffee. There was a dollop of cream on top, shaped like a rosebud. Peter picked up his spoon to stir, but he was asked to wait and watch. He did, and the dollop slowly began to open, a rosebud opening into petals. It was service, it was unique, it was attention to detail, it was showmanship, and it was great.

Next time you order coffee at your local greasy spoon or wait in line more than an hour to check into even a fancy hotel, compare your experience to Peter's. And while you're comparing, think about your customers, your employees, your boss; compare your work to someone else's.

Peter often tells this story—it's one of his favorites. That's the thing about customers; they love to tell other potential customers what they think. They often are your best salespeople.

You can be known as anything, but to be known as the best outweighs everything else. Someone once said that if you buy the best, you will never be sorry. Likewise, if you produce the best, you will never be sorry. There is always a market of people who want the best—who are not satisfied to settle for less.

And even those who are willing to settle will always choose quality if given a choice. Quality works. People intrinsically understand quality, even though it is in essence undefinable. Quality strikes a raw nerve, like an emotion, because quality is from the heart. Quality is real.

My search for the highest-quality goose down brought me not only to China, it also led me to the Hutterite colonies in Montana. The Hutterites are a religious sect that decades ago moved from Germany to Canada and parts of the northern United States to avoid religious persecution. Theirs is a simple life, isolated from the real world by choice. They dress in clothing of a long-ago era: the men in all black, the women in long dresses and bonnets. Except for periodic business with the outside, they keep to themselves, eschewing modern-day life.

The Hutterites live a farming life, producing much of what they eat. When a colony grows too large, a new one is set up in a nearby area. Each colony aims to be self-sufficient—fueled in large part by all the free labor. They eat in communal style, and their homes are simple bungalows. Private property does not exist; everything is owned by the colony.

As part of their self-contained life-style, they raise geese for food. The down is a by-product, which they sell. It is a higher-quality product than Chinese down because the Hutterites let the birds grow 30 to 40 percent longer before killing them. The feathers are a bit larger and fuller, which make the down thicker and work as a better insulator.

I met the Hutterites through one of my relatives, who lived in Montana and years earlier had done some business with them.

When we arrived, they were slaughtering pigs for chops, bacon, sausage, and the like. It was very authentic—blood, innards, the works. It wasn't pretty. Some of the men, all were in black, stopped their work and came to greet me. Others continued to work on the pigs.

It was 10 a.m. when they invited me in and we sat down. I remember the time because that's when they broke out the homemade wine. It was not a Latour, but it wasn't bad. Just a bit early.

I was with the elders, a mostly bearded group of men who had a penchant for speaking among themselves in a German dialect. I tried to follow—I know a bit of German. As soon as they saw I understood a little, they went into a more obscure dialect. At first I felt like an outsider, but then they turned their attention to me. They asked in English what was my opinion of the world goose down situation. They were testing me as a businessman, and—I quickly learned—as a friend.

I told them what I knew, I was honest, and slowly the obscure dialects began to disappear. They smiled—not in general merriment, but directly at me. We had a few more glasses of wine, and they agreed they could sell me some down.

It was almost mystical, like I had been dropped back in time to do business with those from another era—on our monetary terms. I was drinking homemade wine with the bearded elders, and from the room next to us I could hear women singing religious songs in a Germanic tongue. Though women and children were not allowed to talk to me, I saw several peek in at me, the outsider, before they were reprimanded and sent away. The singing next door, I learned, was for a wedding. I was not invited, though I would have loved to have seen it.

The elders offered to take me on a tour of some of the colonies prior to the afternoon discussion of prices.

It was agreed, and we undertook our tour. I drove, since they had few cars. We went to a cafeteria in one of the other colonies. That was where I was pulled aside by some of the more curious young men–they wanted to know about the San Francisco 49ers. Though they were insulated, somehow they still received information. They related to 49ers because the quarterback was Joe Montana, and they lived in Montana. When they brought food, I expected a hearty meal—a natural food treat. Some of it was, but there were also Twinkies and Hostess Ding Dongs. The Hutterites liked junk food! Despite the incongruity, it made sense. The junk foods they used were loaded with preservatives, and the Hutterites made few trips into towns or cities. When they bought food, it had to last. Thus Twinkies.

We returned later to the negotiations and had a spirited time. Quite spirited. We finally settled on a price and terms and celebrated with another glass of homemade wine. This was no mere business transaction; we were friends. I liked them, and they liked me. We could help one another—it was a reason to celebrate.

We kept in touch and visited periodically. It was always the same, a gathering of friends. They even suggested that my wife and I come live there for a while, but we never did. I don't look good in all black, and Margot just isn't the bonnet type.

But that was the beauty of it—they respected who we were, and we respected them. Differences were celebrated even as commonality—the down—caused us to meet.

The Hutterites to me were an adventure, the same as Mt. Everest is to the world's great climbers. It was a pursuit of quality—quality down, a quality relationship, and a disciplined focus on mutual goals.

Discipline is not a bad word. Discipline is not about some schoolmarm with a ruler slapping your fingers, and it's not about the boss threatening to fire you. Discipline is an internal art. It's personal.

For instance, someone in the Walt Disney Company had a dedication to quality and the discipline to carry it out. His concern was that when light bulbs blew out in lamp poles at Disneyland and Disney World, it would be unsafe and did not match the Disney image. That person's attention to detail and expectation of quality led to a computer monitoring system that forecast when a light bulb had ten hours left in it. Now all the bulbs are monitored, and when they reach the ten-hour point, they are replaced. That's quality and discipline.

Quality doesn't come easy. It is the product of absolute focus. There must be a gripping, a tightening of the muscles in pursuit of quality. It is a never-ending quest.

Stanley Marcus of Neiman-Marcus fame tells the story of a friend who knew that most people do not have enough resilience or perseverance to produce a quality product. The man made some of the best ice cream imaginable. One time when Stanley was with his friend, a handful of people asked for the friend's recipe and he gladly gave it away. Stanley was incredulous and asked, "Don't you realize you are giving away the secret of your success?"

The man just smiled. Finally he said, "Stanley, when they see how costly this is and how hard it is to make, they'll never copy me. Never." This parable can be translated to apply to virtually all business today.

As soon as you start producing to price points, there is a tendency to cut quality. When that happens, you don't stand out. The only way to get noticed is to cut prices further, demanding lower costs on your part and most likely lower quality. It's a downward spiral to nowhere. Sometimes cheap is expensive, and expensive is cheap. If you want to revolutionize your market, design first and price later.

Don't misunderstand me—I recognize there is a good market based on low price points. Some companies have done quite well pursuing that strategy. I would argue, however, that the ones that are successful at lower price points are those who also present good quality and give excellent price/value relationships—not those whose sole concern is low price.

Yes, there are limits to the size of top-quality markets. They are, however, steady and reliable markets where there is very little competition.

Quality is what engenders loyalty. The people who lose customers are those who pay no attention to quality. I remember the instant I knew I had to change auto repair shops. I was driving along the freeway, and I happened to glance at the side of the road—the break-down lane. In it was my "skilled" mechanic and his car, a Porsche. He was not working on it. He was yelling at it, cussing it, kicking its fenders. Hell, I could do that.

Someone who is good at what he does—someone who understands quality—would do more than yell. He would examine, measure. Measure, of course, below the bottom line. For the mechanic the bottom line was that the car didn't start. What he should have measured was the efficiency of the car—how it worked. In business efficiency means not only speed but also attention to details. From efficiency comes quality. From details comes efficiency.

Thus, details. Jean Claude Killy knows a bit about precision, about speed, and about attention to details. Killy, the winner of four Olympic gold medals in skiing, showed some friends of mine one day how a champion pays attention to minutiae. They were at Vail—in the back bowls, carving through untracked powder snow. The ski patrol opened it specially for them.

On the first part of the hill, Killy's skiing appeared impeccable. But he was unhappy. "Something is wrong," he said. "Can we try skiing on some moguls and packed snow so I can figure out the problem?" They did. They all flew down the mountain, Jean Claude leading the way. At the bottom of the run everyone was exhilarated—faces flushed, eyes aglow. Except for Jean Claude.

He said again, "Something is wrong." He asked one of my friends, "Do you have a dime?" Killy took off his right boot, took out the leather liner, and removed the plastic foot bed. Under the heel of the foot bed he put the dime—raising the heel a tiny bit. He reassembled the boot and put it back on his foot, declaring the alteration "Perfect!"

And they went off skiing again. In the words of my friend, "You would never have believed it, that a dime could make any difference. But I swear it did, because he was skiing even better than before." Details—any little edge.

Killy knows how to get a little edge—attention to details. He also knows how to get a big edge—hard work. Combine the two and a large dose of inspiration, and you have the makings of a champion.

Quality is as much an abstract feeling as it is a quantifiable aspect of a product. It is like a warm glow where the spinal cord touches the brain—a surreal yet physical feeling that says, "This is good." As Robert M. Pirsig wrote in *Zen & the Art of Motorcycle Maintenance*, "Quality is not a thing. It is an event."

Indeed it is, and the Ruby Mountain Heli Ski Company

of northern Nevada runs some great events. It is an owner-operated company, not some division of another division of some conglomerate. And it is prosperous.

They fly small helicopters (they call them "ships") up into the mountains. There is a pilot, a guide, and three to four passengers. The idea is to create intimacy—a connection of experience among a small group of friends. The intimacy is maintained when the people go skiing, with the same ratio between guides and skiers.

The runs are sensational—1,500 to 2,500 vertical feet through light, knee-deep powder in the midst of the spectacular Ruby Mountains. It is one of those spots in the world—and there are many, if you just look—where nature seems to be almost a temple to perfection. Quality is certainly the feeling given off by nature at her grandest.

But it doesn't just happen—the Ruby people must work hard to get the skiers on the hills. The ski runs for the paying guests begin from 6:30 a.m. to 7 a.m. The guides' day begins earlier, at the first sign of light—5 a.m. or so. They go out by helicopter and check the safety and viability of the ski conditions. When there is concern about potential avalanches, they ease their doubts by throwing explosive charges to set the avalanches off. They scour the hills for the best and safest conditions. The customers generally have no idea of the two hours of preparatory activity. To them the adventure is magic.

But the owners of Ruby Mountain Heli Ski understand what it takes to make magic. They understand quality. In heli-skiing, safety is the first thing. Always. All skiers are fitted with a homing device to help find them in case of an avalanche. And all are trained in avalanche survival, even if they have already been trained elsewhere.

Safety is always on the owners' minds, but it is not the

only concern. They want to maximize the skiing for their customers—they aim to create great adventures. For the customer it "just happens." But the people at R.M.H.S. know that nothing of quality ever just happens—it takes hard work, dedication, and, of course, attention to details.

When the sky is not safe for flying, in fog or blizzard conditions, they use snow cats, mechanical vehicles that can transport people up the steep hills in the worst of snow conditions. From a cost standpoint it is much more costly to maintain both helicopters and snow cats to take skiers into the mountains. But on bad days there will be no waiting for the skies to clear. The skiers won't get quite as many vertical feet of skiing in using the snow cats, but they still get a tremendous amount and won't have to miss a precious day. Of course, it more than earns back the cost to the Ruby Mountain people because the skiers have the adventure of their lives and tell everyone they know about it. Positive word-of-mouth advertising is always the strongest advertising.

They even offer alternative lodging to satisfy different personalities. They operate out of an old farmhouse in Lamoille, Nevada. It's a small town, not near much other than the Ruby Mountains. The farmhouse is cozy—a warm, mountain throwback to a simpler time. When you look around, you expect to smell an apple pie baking in the oven—it feels *that* way.

Most who go heli-skiing with Ruby stay at the farmhouse and enjoy the hearty meals and the collegial atmosphere.

Some might find too much camaraderie confining. Some wish for some time alone during this most spectacular adventure. The owners have arranged it so those souls can stay at a nearby motel as an alternative. The choice is yet another nice touch—one of individuality. The owners of Ruby Mountain Heli Ski understand more than just business. They understand people.

They understand that quality is not a halfway proposition—it is a full-time occupation. To get it requires honest effort—100 percent commitment. Partway doesn't cut it. You have to go all the way. When you do, the rewards are enormous.

Quality sells. Quality works. A reputation for quality is incredibly marketable. But of course, it doesn't stagnate—quality, like life, is fluid.

For quality to sell there has to be a strong subjective agreement among your customers. For instance, I once told one of my board members who ran a major U.S. pizza chain that I knew how to instantly double his business. Needless to say, he was curious. I acknowledged his company had superb locations, tremendous advertising, and great prices. But, I explained, there was one thing missing—good pizza. Customers came once because of the MBA stuff—location, advertising, and prices. But they would only return if the company got down to the basics of what the business was really about—a quality product. Make a good pizza, I said, and you'll get the customers to come back and buy a second pizza.

Not long thereafter he sold the company to a conglomerate for a handsome profit—leaving the worries of quality to the new owners.

Going all the way for quality really means exactly that. All aspects of your business must be focused on quality. If they aren't, somewhere, inevitably, there will be failings. The way a receptionist greets someone is just as important as the way a production worker performs. From the logo to the company cafeteria, it all counts toward creating an aura of quality.

Somerset Maugham, in *The Mixture Before*, said it well: "It is a funny thing about life. If you refuse to accept anything but the best, very often you get it."

At The North Face a major, ongoing discussion was whether we should use the word "high," "higher," or "highest" in our business definition of our quality. Over the course of our company history, this was perhaps our most famous discussion. It always came up, perhaps because I always brought it up.

Despite its repetitive nature I encouraged the discussion every time we held a long-range planning meeting. Some advocated "high" or "higher" because they wanted precise, quantifiable, and reachable goals. A few of us always argued for "highest" because we knew the only thing that kept us in business was constantly having higher quality than our competition. We *had* to be the best.

As a goal the highest quality represents a moving target that can never be quantified or reached. This can be frustrating to some. But to those with vision it is a tremendous guiding beacon. What it says is, if a product can be made better, it must and will be made better by us.

This can sometimes be disruptive to continuity and short-term efficiency. At The North Face if a new technology or new material came along that was better than our own, we would change. There was a short-term cost. But the long-term reward was stability and growth.

Our entire focus was quality. It was our religion, and we were evangelists. We knew it was what differentiated us from our competitors. We wanted our dealers to know it too, so one year we put together a seminar based solely on quality—quality of the future. We called it Future Q.

We invited our dealers from all over the world to come to Berkeley to talk about quality. This was more than meeting with dealers; it was corporate scholarship. We felt we could learn from our dealers, and they from us. We wanted an exchange of information and ideas.

I saw the seminar as a chance to nourish quality. To talk about it, think about it, dream about it, and experience it. We knew that from the discussion would come an improved reality.

It was wonderful—a celebration of life at its most potent. We had meals based on the concept "Future and Quality." We had speakers, such as Peter Glen and myself. We played games. We had fun.

We divided the participants into groups and sent them into San Francisco on an "Idea Search." They were to come back with the best ideas they saw in retail. They were to find ideas they could take back to their companies, ideas that cost no more than $25 to implement.

Our dealers came up with several wonderful ideas which we used. One was to expand the lighting in the back of the stores. The back of the store is always the least well trafficked area with the lowest sales per square foot. By increasing wattage, changing color schemes, or using windows, retailers were able to attract more customers to the back, and let them spend more time pleasurably in the stores.

Another idea was to alternate the direction of hangers on the clothing racks at the front of the store. This prevented shoplifters from snatching an armful of merchandise and running off.

By taking the dealers to our stores and openly discussing the facts of our business, good and bad, we all learned and became more imbued with the concept of quality. There was tremendous individual growth. And there was more;

there was business growth. Our dealer loyalty soared. Many dealers immediately improved the visual merchandising and operations of their stores as a result of the seminar. This translated into greatly improved sales and profits. And the best part was everyone had a good time. Quality, unquestionably, is fun.

In some companies, however, quality is not a guiding concept; it is merely a public relations slogan. It has no meaning because there is nothing behind it. There is no care, no commitment. The product isn't the best—it's maybe okay. The people who make it do it solely for money. Even the people who buy it don't expect much. They have been beaten down by bad products.

Eventually, though, customers change companies. Even the most timid customers—though uncomplaining—will begin to vote with their feet. Everyone wants something of quality.

There is one way to tell people up front of your commitment to highest quality. It is the best way—a full and complete warranty. A lifetime warranty.

For one thing, a warranty gives you an easy way to quantify quality—just measure the returns on warranty. It's not perfectly accurate, but it's a start. An even better way to quantify quality is counting the number of defects produced that never go to market. Many companies believe that if defects go down the company is improving. My experience is different. I believe every company produces some defects; that is the nature of production and the nature of business. If you don't acknowledge the defects and cull them out, they don't go away. They probably go to your customers, who will then either create returns or, far worse, vote with their feet and begin buying from another company.

Yet lawyers and vulture capitalists will tell you that you

are crazy to consider a lifetime warranty on anything. They are wrong!

A full warranty sends a profound message—it says you will back the product forever. Not many companies use that strategy, but those that do are almost always successful.

Ironically, with a full warranty some of your best reputation comes when you have major problems. People doubt quality so much that they never really believe what you say with your warranty until you prove it. When you do honor your obligation and treat your customer right, it is so unusual that the customer becomes a vociferous spokesperson for your company.

When Gore-tex Fabrics introduced a new waterproof, breathable fabric, it revolutionized the business of outerwear and sports clothing. It was a success from the start—functional, high priced, but without competition. For years people had been looking for the product they created. It was the highest known quality.

But there was a problem. A year after it was introduced, the new material, which was laminated to standard commercial fabric, began to bubble and separate. In the fashion-conscious world of outdoor clothing, the product was a loser. Even more important from a quality point of view, the separation caused the clothing to lose some of its function—the garment didn't keep its owner as dry as before the problem started.

It was a potential disaster. But Gore immediately put its R&D people to work and they developed what they called Generation II Gore-tex. The company then offered to replace every garment that failed. Every one. And they lived up to their promise.

The customers were ecstatic. Gore-tex reached an unassailable quality and ethical pinnacle. Even when the competition developed similar waterproof, breathable products at lower price points, they couldn't overtake Gore. The company continues to lead the waterproof, breathable fabric market. Their product unquestionably meets the test of being the highest quality. And every day they are working to improve even that.

When The North Face launched its line of ski wear in 1980, we had the perfect plan. But what we learned is that a plan is just a word without the right product.

The right product for The North Face was, of course, to have the very best outerwear in the world. We knew how to do it—we had the technology. But we were also naive about the difficulty of being the best in ski wear. We knew it would be hard. We didn't know how hard.

We did great research and had a totally revolutionary product—ski wear that stood up to the cold, wind, sun, and abuse. Layers of clothing that worked combined or alone—in different altitudes and in different kinds of weather. Behind this, we had total assurance from our fabric suppliers that their materials could do what we said they could do.

Our plan was to outfit the ski instructors at Vail. It went like this: They'd get the outfits for a nominal fee and be happy because the product was the best. We'd get positive publicity because all winter long skiers at Vail would see the instructors in The North Face ski wear—word of mouth goes fast in such small enclaves as Vail. Good skiers in good equipment. Great idea.

There was a problem. You see, when good-skiers-in-good-equipment become good-skiers-in-*bad*-equipment, you've got a real problem. By the end of the first season at Vail, all the outfits of the instructors were deteriorating from the sun's ultraviolet rays on the mountain—they started looking like cheap sharkskin suits.

You know what we had on all that equipment? We had our lifetime warranty on all that equipment. And we had a fabric supplier who refused to back us up. Basically we had asked the supplier if they could make fabric that would hold up to the sun, and they said yes. So we went forward.

And when it didn't work, the supplier refused any help other than an offer of $1,000 toward an ad with their company name in it. Hell of a guy. I'll never forget it.

As a result we wrote off more than $100,000 by taking every piece back and replacing them with new, workable garments made from fabric from another supplier. That was a huge amount for a company our size.

And you know what? It was without a doubt one of the best things we ever did. Vail was ecstatic with the replacement product. The people at Vail were so amazed that we actually lived up to our warranty that they became vocal advocates for our company.

The North Face is now the U.S. volume leader in the market of highest-quality functional ski-wear for serious skiers. In fact, in 20 years the cost of our warranty rebates for all of our products never exceeded 1 percent of our sales. Sure, we had blips like the Vail situation. But all in all, I can honestly say we couldn't have afforded not to back our products with a full warranty.

I don't ever want to apologize for my product, but if I have to, I will. That is a statement of commitment.

In fact, our warranty and repair department became so famous for its work that it broadcast the quality of the company. We repaired sleeping bags on which people had put hot skillets and backpacks that bears had chewed on. The work was good, efficient, and fair. If the fault was even remotely ours, we would repair or replace the product for free. If it was the customer's fault, we would charge only a modest fee. Our goal was to make them happy.

One day a customer came in with a Sierra Designs sleeping bag—ironically, a company we would later acquire. The customer said. "I hear you do the best and fastest repair work. I bought this at Sierra Designs, but they tell me they can't repair it for three weeks. I need it now for my vacation. Can you repair it? For free?" The customer claimed he didn't have any money for the repair, since he needed it for his vacation. "Maybe you can get the money back from Sierra Designs," suggested the customer.

The warranty and repair department decided to do the work for free. Their reasoning, which I totally supported when I later learned of it, was that the cost of the repair was minimal. The person would be so delighted about the repair (even though he was clearly scamming us) and so positive about our company that he would be sure to tell everyone he knew. It would be infinitely more effective than any advertisement we could ever put out.

A full warranty also works on customers on a subliminal level—they realize you can't afford many errors like the one they just experienced and stay in business. A full warranty telegraphs the message that you are serious about quality.

The concept behind a strong warranty works as well inside a company as it does with your customers. It provides clarity, simplicity, and focus. It sets a clear policy for dealing with customers and a guideline for everyone, from switchboard operators to designers. It is a story that can be easily and swiftly communicated to all employees: We make only the best. It is a policy that personally involves everyone. As a result attitudes are buoyed and employees become positive salespeople for your company.

A full warranty says you understand quality as a goal

and as an idea. As a goal, quality is tied in to hard work, inspiration, dedication, and fun. As an idea quality is a harder call. Should one aim for the highest quality? If so, isn't it unattainable? Is quality a final aim or one of a vital, continuous state of being? A full warranty tells the buyer that quality is fluid—it must always be there.

All of these words pile up now—words such as focus and fluid and perseverance and instinct and resilience and discipline. On and on goes the list. But what does it mean? What does it mean, finally, when you get past all the verbal barriers?

Quality is joy. That's what it means. In the midst of all the hard work quality is laughter with a friend on the path to mutual accomplishment. Quality, quite simply, is the best.

10

SHARING VISIONS:
When Leaders Lead

But then they danced down the street like dingledodies, and I shambled after as I've been doing all my life after the people who interest me, because the only people for me are the mad ones, the ones who are mad to live, mad to talk, mad to be saved, desirous of everything at the same time, the ones who never yawn or say a commonplace thing, but burn, burn, burn like fabulous yellow roman candles exploding like spiders across the stars and in the middle you see the blue centerlight pop and everybody goes, "Awww!"

—Jack Kerouac, *On the Road*

Dingledodies live! I've worked with them and I know, as Kerouac knew, that the mad ones are the ones who buy into the dream with the deepest fervor. The dream of life. A leader's job is to share his version of that same dream and then rally the talents and energies of everyone toward the cause.

There is nothing more energizing than talent—plugged-in talent. The electric ones are the ones whose leadership aims to incite. When the light is bright enough, it can create work that is not only moving but also inspiring. Ernest

Hemingway's *A Farewell to Arms* had that effect on Edward Hope, a reviewer with the *New York Herald-Tribune*. Hope was so moved by Hemingway's tale of love and war on the World War I Italian front that he wrote: "It is one of those things—like the Grand Canyon—that one doesn't care to talk about. It is so great a book that praise of it sounds like empty babbling."

And so it is with praise of the human spirit. It sounds like empty babbling, but—dingledodies live!

For the last 25 years or so I have watched, dumbfounded, as much of American business has flailed about aimlessly in the singular pursuit of profits. Executives disconnected themselves from everyone as they spent every spare moment weaving their private cocoons. It was almost funny, almost like the fable of the emperor's new clothes, as I watched the business fabric of jargon, titles, and prejudice unravel. Beyond the pretentious audacity to employees, and in fact to the rest of the world, it was, simply, a disgrace.

I'm fed up with shoddy quality and service and incompetent people doing nothing more than trying to hold on to their jobs. I'm angry with the lack of energy and pride. I'm tired of old excuses, and I'm bored with "new and improved" when it means nothing.

I'm too competitive to accept playing dead to global competition, particularly when it is clear to me there is nothing—and everything—magical to running a business. It is about common sense, the ability to think logically *and* emotionally. That's all. It's about quality, about digging past the layers of bullshit most organizations pretend exist and finding humanity. It's easy to do and more than worth the effort.

You have to look at more than profits if you want to be a leader. You have to actually care about your company and the people in the company. Leading requires passionately immersing yourself in a deep vision of the future. Leading means creating the future, creating more light than heat.

Leading means making connections, both for yourself and your company. You want people to identify with the company and its mission so that there is a bond. It is a winning, home-team attitude—like that of Harley Davidson, with perhaps the most loyal customers in the world.

Every company has its own culture. There are many types, but the best revolves around fun and humor. Business, after all, is the theater of the absurd—a potpourri of laughter for those who connect to the vision.

Connections are always individual events, even when the leader leads thousands. And in the increasingly global world (if that makes sense), leaders sometimes must communicate with three or more continents in one day. Leaders now must make electronic connections to the masses and yet the goal must be the same—to touch individuals personally. It is ever more difficult to go beyond the mechanical connection to the human one.

True leaders revel in individuality—their own and their employees'. They allow employees freedom within the boundaries of fairness. Leaders recognize and honor each human spirit they meet. They revel in the energy and potential. They start with themselves.

Galen Rowell, the photographer, is famous for his pictures using morning and evening light. He is famous for a good reason—he takes great photos. On one adventure he was in Tibet to take pictures of the Potalla, the Dalai Lama's residence. He wanted to do it in his signature way—at sunset. He began his arduous ascent in the late morning, hiking to locations where he could best photograph the Potalla. The altitude was between 12,000 and 13,000 feet—

sorry-lung altitude. Certainly not the easiest place to hike or run.

Just as the sun was going down, it started to rain. Galen saw a rainbow. He figured out that if he ran about a mile up and to his left, he could take a picture of the rainbow exactly over the Dalai Lama's palace.

So he ran.

And he ran.

And he ran. You possibly saw the picture. It's been published all over. Your first reaction may have been, "What a great shot! Was that photographer lucky!" Lucky, yes. He's worked so hard he's been lucky hundreds of times.

Galen Rowell is a leader in his field. He is among the very best outdoor photographers in the world—meeting an internal challenge to be a leader to himself.

From the spark that ignites will, leadership creates a vision and shares it with others. When the vision is accepted and shared, a human will can accomplish almost anything. Focus and direct—quality will come forth.

In the early 1950s Sapporo, Japan, was a cold and isolated city. On the northernmost island of Japan, where winds whip in from Siberia, Sapparo's winters were a study in monotony and depression. The economy was depressed. There was nothing for the residents to do but burrow themselves in their homes. Some stewed, but others dreamed.

Every winter it was the same—isolation. The cold was a fact; the Siberian winds to many were a curse. But the Sapporo civic leaders in the early 1950s had a most radical idea—to stop vilifying the weather and celebrate it. The idea was to celebrate in the cold and create an event unique to Sapporo. They did this by creating the Yuki Matsuri Festival, a celebration of snow and ice sculpture.

It started small. At first it was a local event, designed

mainly to enliven the spirits of the locals. But it grew swiftly. Word quickly spread that people were having fun in the dead of winter in Sapporo. Newspapers printed pictures of the spectacular sculptures carved for the festival. Artists began planning their year around the event.

It is an incredible sight, with hundreds of snow and ice sculptures—some as large as five-story buildings. But the large sculptures are no mere artistic feat; they require the skills of world-class ice climbers as well as the talent of sculptors. The sculptures vary greatly in size and design. There are replicas of fierce warriors, castles, mythical characters, and whatever else the artists' imaginations conjure up. The festival has continued to this day.

In recent years more than two million people have visited the annual festival—toasting the sculptures with sake and joyously spending their money in Sapporo.

A shared vision is a wonderful thing. It doesn't just happen; the shared vision emanates from an individual vision. It is molded into a shared vision when a leader takes action and motivates others to also take action.

In Sapporo civic leaders were faced with a depressing situation—terrible weather, monotony, and economic doldrums. They turned it around because they had a vision of how to change it. With that vision they were able to get the city to buy into their dream of an ice festival. United, the people of Sapporo created magic.

The start of cubism in the art world exemplifies the evolution of a shared vision. In the early 1900s Pablo Picasso was a Spanish artist living in the impoverished artist colony in the Montparnasse section of Paris. It was there that he met and befriended French artist Georges Braque.

They made a connection. Despite their differences in nationality, they had much in common. It was a friendship based on energy and inspiration. It was a friendship that would change the art world.

For countless hours the two young artists would talk—meeting at cafés, bistros, and tabacs, observing colors, people, and societal changes. Picasso was enthralled with Braque. He called him "Wilbur"—a high compliment, naming him after Wilbur Wright, the inventor of the airplane.

From his immersion in the frenetic urban petri dish of Paris, Picasso sensed a fundamental shift in society—from the stability of the mid-19th century to the frenzy of modern society. He and Braque talked endlessly about this, both understanding that they were in the midst of the dawning of a new age. They agreed that art was going to reflect that change, and they set out to be the creators of the new form.

Individually they painted. Collectively they talked and explored the shifting scene in Paris. The gray-brown colors of the world they lived in—a world of cobblestones and smoky bars—replaced the pastel colors used by the earlier Impressionists. The soft, simple landscapes and still lifes dealing with depth, light, and shading gave way to multiple impressions—impressions that shifted, overlapped, and relied on flat planes. Cubism appeared to be composed of work that was almost cut and reassembled—perhaps a reflection of what Braque and Picasso felt modern society was doing to the traditions of the former century.

Through this transition Braque and Picasso moved in concert. As Braque said in describing that period, "We were like two mountaineers roped together." When sand was added for texture, both added it at exactly the same time. When stenciled commercial lettering appeared in Picasso's work, it also appeared in Braque's. The colors were the same, the textures were the same, and the angles and techniques were the same. Theirs was a shared vision of the highest order—an almost metaphysical union of two very diverse souls.

Yet it was competitive. Studies have discovered that there was a tremendous rivalry going on, especially on the part of Picasso. It was an open rivalry, but fierce just the same. They shared ideas. They shared perspective. They each had access to the other's studio and work in progress. They pushed limits.

When the first cubist paintings by Picasso and Braque came out in 1910 and 1911, they looked virtually identical. Today art museums put them side by side for effect and you cannot tell the difference. The book *Modern Art*, by Sam Hunter and John Jacobus, explains that "the artistic relationship between Picasso and Braque [was] so close that in the absence of signatures—and they very rarely signed or dated their works at the time—it is almost impossible to determine who made which individual contribution to the evolution of the cubist style."

Braque and Picasso comprehended and thrived on the competition. Although Braque early on was the more famous painter, Picasso fairly quickly eclipsed him. That should be the goal of business—to motivate everyone to compete with the strength of their individuality toward a mutually energizing goal.

Sharing a vision with a lot of followers becomes geometrically more difficult, but also geometrically more powerful. The importance of the vision, like the use of symbols, gains as the numbers grow. Vision is what sustains the effort during the silent times in a company.

At The North Face, where vision was the heart of our business, our vision was one of quality. It was woven (we thought literally) into the fabric of our business. Above and beyond everything else, we wanted to be the best. It was not some minor goal that would be nice to meet—it was, as I saw it, our reason for living.

We had no desire to make everyone in the company like our plan. Quite the opposite. We wanted to make the plan, and the sacrifices necessary, so clear that those who were not in tune with it would quit, recognizing that it was time for them to move on.

In situations where employees didn't fit but also didn't have the fortitude to move on, the best solution was to quietly fire them. Just as surgery, even radical surgery, can lead to better health, removing people who don't share the vision of the company can improve the company's health. In such situations we helped ease their transition out of the company. Everyone who remained was happier, and the shared vision was stronger.

Shared visions don't just happen. They must be nurtured. In a company the best way to do this is to create reasons for people to get together on a regular basis. The most obvious, yet probably worst way is with meetings. They don't work because they are not really interactive, and often no one listens. Meetings foster power games and hierarchy, which undermine passion and communication.

Informal gatherings are better. You can schedule events around company anniversaries, picnics, corporate sporting teams, or Friday afternoon happy hours. The idea is to get people talking to each other—not "onstage" for each other, but onstage together. Sharing visions, if you will. People have to be passionate *and* they have to connect.

Alice Waters had a vision, a sweeping vision. She put together a team that turned that vision into reality—one of the best restaurants in the United States. Waters's vision was to create a whole new style of cooking, and she did so at her restaurant, Chez Panisse, in Berkeley.

In her view food is more than sustenance—it's pleasure. Her food stresses the California virtues of constant farm-fresh produce, and her restaurants stress food that is creative, healthy, and generally without additives. It is no longer just her vision. It is now known throughout the world as California Cuisine.

Instead of opening one restaurant at Chez Panisse, she opened two. Downstairs is a formal restaurant (or as formal as one might get in Berkeley), serving one set dinner menu at a fixed price. Never in the 20-plus-year history of the restaurant has it served the same meal twice. Upstairs she has a second restaurant—a more casual café with a constantly changing, extensive menu that includes everything from farm-fresh goat cheese salads to nasturium-garnished pizza.

Hers was a revolutionary vision, not an evolutionary one. She has extensive knowledge of French cooking and she certainly pays homage to it. But her vision is uniquely American, uniquely Californian, and uniquely Alice and her fine team of chefs.

To effect her vision she had to break a lot of the traditions of the restaurant business—doing things in absolutely new ways, often risky, which dictated a lot of extraordinary effort. And it required convincing a lot of people to do things they had never done before.

Waters loved the goat cheese she had tasted in France, but she couldn't find it fresh in the United States. No problem. She convinced one of her friends to share her vision and develop a goat farm north of San Francisco, in Sonoma. The goat farm is now a great success in its own right—serving Chez Panisse and a myriad of California cuisine restaurants in northern California.

Waters started Chez Panisse in a converted old, dark

wooden two-story house in a weak retail section of Berkeley. There is no parking, and no noticeable signage. But her vision was so strong that it worked anyway—for the last ten years it has been ranked in the top ten American restaurants by virtually every reviewer in the United States. Many rank it at number one or two.

Her advertising is equally unique. It uses none of the standard advertising vehicles, only a different poster each year celebrating Chez Panisse's anniversary. The poster has always been designed by David Lance Goines. At first, the story has it, Waters traded meals for his work. But he became as successful as she did, and his poster art is now world famous. Their relationship has never been based on the written contract, but rather on the strength of their human connection. Waters compensates Goines with more than free meals presently, but they still work together as they did in the early days—recognizing the magic of their shared vision.

Her vision was a detailed one, requiring many others to commit to it. Besides seeking a different cheese, she also required farm-fresh produce and meats with no pesticides or synthetic hormones. To acquire these she convinced a number of farmers to produce them, even if it was for her restaurant's singular consumption. She got her way, as even more people shared her vision.

Probably the most amazing part of her success is that she turned the age-old restaurant problem of high turnover among chefs into an asset. Instead of trying to bind them with some form of "golden handcuffs," which are so traditional in the business world, she accepted turnover as inevitable. It was a chance for her to learn from her chefs, just as they learned from her. This fueled her need for constant change and encouraged some of the world's best chefs to come to her—chefs like Jeremiah Tower of STARS and Mark Miller of the Coyote Cafe who, in their own right, have gone on to revolutionize the restaurant and food industry.

Machievelli said, "Make no small plans . . . for they have not the power to stir men's blood." Human passion is aroused by the pursuit of greatness. People will work for money—but they'll give *everything* they have if they believe. Leadership has to touch that which makes a spirit soar. Great leadership creates not just vision, but grand vision.

The 3,300-foot sheer rock face of Mt. Thor in Auyuittuq National Park in Canada presented such a grand vision to Steve Holmes. Holmes was consumed by his vision—a deeply personal one in which he wanted to rappel down Mt. Thor for a new world rappeling record. And then, equally as daring, he wanted to climb back up the sheer stone on the same rope.

The prior record for rappeling had been down the stone monolith El Capitan in Yosemite Valley—about 700 feet less than Holmes's proposed Mt. Thor attempt.

It was his passion. And it was his quest. He quit his job and sold all his belongings to finance the trip. He was consumed by fitness, understanding the importance of an in-tune body to make his dream a reality. He began to piece together a team.

Holmes's team, it turned out, was mostly spelunkers—those who explore caves. Spelunkers are more used to making descents than mountaineers. Mountaineers generally think first about climbing, not descending, so Holmes doubted they'd be properly enthused about his plan.

Among his team was photographer Nick Nichols, the man from Chapter 8 who got thrown around by gorillas.

Holmes knew of Nichols's exploits. He knew Nichols had a full-blooded passion.

Holmes began selecting his team. The idea was not just to get some people who were willing to go along on the excursion, but to find true believers—those who understood and shared his passion. He wanted people who would guarantee success.

He found ten people, ten souls with a flame as bright as his own. They began to plan as a team and expand the vision. Because the assault on Mt. Thor was an excursion that had never been done before, he and his team had to dream up new equipment. Once the vision was refined and detailed to his satisfaction, Holmes had to share his vision even further, with the corporate world. In one case he needed a mile-long mountaineering rope. He found a company to make it. He needed other equipment, things not available on the commercial market—which he had to design himself. Things such as special rappeling equipment and climbing ascendors (climbing ascendors are mechanical devices that allow climbers to climb up the rope, but not slide down.) Each time he had to share his vision to convince companies to build the unique equipment he needed. In every case the company became excited about being involved. His passion was contagious. I know—The North Face even designed some of the clothing to protect his team from the cold, damp, and variable weather of northern Canada.

The rappel was almost like a free-fall—thrilling and frightening. The climb back up, equivalent in distance to three World Trade Towers in New York City, was exhausting. Twenty-five minutes to get to the bottom, but more than five hours to climb back to the top. And why?

Because it was worth it, because each of the participants believed fully that life is for living, not watching. They believed that a grand vision was something they wanted to share. Steve Holmes had a vision of a world record and of the thrill of a lifetime. He shared that vision, and it became reality. Steve Holmes knows what it is to lead. He knows what it is to share vision. He has proved it on the face of Mt. Thor.

To lead is to personalize, to inspire people at their core. You must get others to share a common view—viscerally as well as intellectually. That sharing can be with one person or with many, but the concept is the same. A shared vision must not be stagnant; it must evolve. A vision that works especially well becomes not the product of one person, but of all involved. As the Chinese philosopher Lao-tzu said 2,500 years ago, "True leaders inspire people to do great things and, when the work is done, their people proudly say, 'We did this ourselves.'"

Vision is active, not passive. You must open your senses and your mind to the world around you and periodically indulge your fantasies of the future.

Climbers know they will never make it to the peak unless they have already been there in their minds. It is the same in business. Commit yourself to your people and constantly communicate with them in a simple and honest manner. Let them know where your heart lies—fulfill your commitments. Set an example by committing your full body and soul to the task you undertake. Visualize success and communicate it. Talk *and* listen. Listen and talk. If someone shares your vision, he or she can probably improve it.

Leadership at its best is not a chore. It is a wonderful, exhilarating adventure—a voyage fueled by human potential. It is frantic at times, almost manic—like a 100-yard dash rather than a stroll in the park. It is urgent. It is about tapping into the source of power inside each human soul and getting it to care about something that you find important.

That is the key—you must find your vision important. Holmes did. Everyone I have written about in this book did. I did. I believe in the depths of my soul that it is important to be the very best in the world. At The North Face, I knew my vision was about much more than making tents, backpacks, and ski clothing. It was about measuring up—looking in the mirror and feeling at peace with myself. My vision was about making a difference; that's the measure I used. I wanted to matter in people's lives. And you?

What I'm calling for is a revolt—a revolt of honesty—both against those pompous incompetents with titles and for the power of vision. It is time to stop the bitching and get on with the business of changing. Speak up. Act out. If your company is so afraid of your ideas that it won't listen—or worse, condescends—then you should quit and move on.

Don't take it anymore. You don't have to. Find a better job, one where the company appreciates your leadership. Someone somewhere has a vision you can share. You just have to find it.

Or you can create it. Start your own business. Find something you love and make it your life's work. When an artist dies, the artist leaves behind "a body of work." Do the same—begin your body of work. Find a vision and share it with others. Don't just stand back and let it all be. Live. Burn. Dance like a dingledodie.